CALIFORNIA'S TOP TEN RESTAURANTS

AND 266 OTHER GREAT PLACES TO EAT THAT DON'T RIP YOU OFF !

By

Raye and Bob Herzbrun

Armstrong Publishing Co.

Los Angeles, Calif.

Many thanks to Marjorie R. Thomas and Peter Hannaford for their splendid contributions and good taste.

CALIFORNIA'S TOP TEN RESTAURANTS / And 266 Other
Great Places to Eat That Don't Rip You Off!
by Raye and Bob Herzbrun

First Printing, October 1977
Copyright © 1977 by Armstrong Publishing Company
Library of Congress Catalog Card Number: 77-077904
ISBN: 0-915936-04-6
All rights reserved.
Printed in the United States of America

Designed By: Augie Rinaldi

Published By: Armstrong Publishing Company
                 5514 Wilshire Boulevard
                 Los Angeles, California 90036
                 (213) 937-3600

CONTENTS

WHAT THIS BOOK IS ALL ABOUT... AND HOW TO USE IT TO LOCATE TOP RESTAURANTS IN CALIFORNIA WITHOUT HASSLE OR BANKRUPTCY

The "Top Ten Book of California Restaurants" is a new kind of restaurant guide. Instead of the usual alphabetical listings, the "Top Ten Book" organizes restaurants the same way you probably do, when picking a place to dine.

First, restaurants are grouped by geographical location. (Where do you want to eat?) Then they are grouped by type of restaurant within each area—French, Italian, Oriental, snack etc. (What do you want to eat?) Third, each restaurant is identified by price range. (How much do you want to spend?) Finally, only *"top" restaurants are included,* which means your time and dining dollars can be concentrated on those places which really give you something for your money.

"Ten Top Restaurants" have been selected in each grouping. Which, of course, is where the "Top Ten Book of California Restaurants" gets its name. Actually, the book could also be called the "Top 276 Book of California Restaurants," because that's the total number of eating and drinking places included ...276 restaurants. But organizing them into "Top Ten" by groups is what makes this book so easy to use.

Now, what is a "top" restaurant?

"Tops" to one person may not be "tops" to another... because different people have different tastes. (Which is a very good thing. If everyone liked the same restaurant, think how crowded it would be.)

We feel a "top" restaurant is one which is "tops" at doing what it sets out to do. It doesn't have to be expensive, or formal, or serve exotic dishes. A "top" restaurant is one which does its thing very well — whether it be classic French or hamburgers, salad Nicoise or salad bar, silver service or plastic and paper.

For our taste, a top restaurant is much more than food alone. It's the total dining experience—food, service, hospitality, atmosphere, cleanliness and value. "Did we have a good time?" "Did they make us feel good?" "Did we get our money's worth?" These are the things which make a restaurant "tops"...and the things we looked for in selecting "Top Ten" restaurants.

Does the "Top Ten Book" include all the top restaurants in California? No, it does not. In many categories there are a large number of good restaurants to choose from. And when concentrating on ten, some good ones had to be passed up.

Every place that is included, however, is a top restaurant ...
based on our taste and experience.

In boiling the list down to a "top ten" in each category, we used several criteria. We picked restaurants in different sections of each city. And we picked them in different price ranges. So whatever your dining mood — menu, atmosphere, location, price — you should find one that's "just right" among the "Top Ten."

And always, we picked restaurants which "don't rip you off." Does that mean this is a book of inexpensive restaurants? Absolutely not ... although the book includes many that are lower priced. What it means is that in our experience, every restaurant which has been included gives you value for your money ... whether it be an intensive service French dinner house or a corner hamburger stand. (Yes, the "Top Ten Book" includes both.)

One final note on selecting "Top Ten" restaurants: you'll find we not only included established restaurants which are now at their peak, but many new restaurants which are already good, and getting better. As a result, instead of the same old list of restaurants which have been appearing in guide books for years, you'll find the "Top Ten Book" includes many places which are different and unusual ... "top" restaurants for a new dining experience.

Except for the Top Restaurants of California, which have been selected "one through ten," all restaurants are listed alphabetically within their "Top Ten" groupings.

A QUICK REVIEW OF "TOP TEN" LANGUAGE

Most of the terminology used in this book is self-explanatory, but a few words need clarification.

CLASSIFICATION OF RESTAURANTS

Oriental Restaurants include Chinese, Japanese, Korean and Thai. Each restaurant listed is identified by the particular style of cooking which is featured.

International Restaurants is a "catch all" category for food from various parts of the world not covered elsewhere in the book. For instance, Mexican, Philippine, Greek, Afghan, Indian, Russian, Etc.

Soups, Salads, Sandwiches, Snacks and Suppers. What more can we say? They're tops when you want a light meal.

Good Deal Restaurants are not necessarily cheapies, but offer outstanding value.

Special Interest Restaurants offer a "special attraction" in addition to the dining experience.

PRICE RANGE must be defined because what is "moderate" to one person is "expensive" to another. The "dollar price" listed next to the price ranges below is for a typical dinner. FOOD ONLY. Cocktails, wine, beer, taxes, tip and such will be extra. Prices may be a bit less if you scrimp. Or more, if you're a big spender. Also, remember prices do change. But the range gives you an idea of what to expect.

TYPICAL DINNER — FOOD ONLY
(Cocktails, wine, tip and tax will be extra)
Lower Priced — Under $6 per person.
Moderate — $6 to $10 per person.
Expensive — $10 to $15 per person.
Very Expensive — Over $15 per person.

CREDIT CARDS are noted by the initials you're familiar with — except for BankAmericard which is now changing to VISA, so is shown as V(BA). Others are AE: American Express, CB: Carte Blanche, DC: Diner's Club, MC: Master Charge. "Major Cards" means most of the above and, at the very least, AE, MC and V(BA).

• • •

It is estimated there are 45,000 restaurants in California. This book is *not* about 44,724 of them. It is about the other 276 which we call "tops." Enjoy them.

Raye and Bob Herzbrun

ABOUT THE AUTHORS....

Raye and Bob Herzbrun have been researching, reviewing and reporting on the restaurants of California for many years. They're best known as founder/editors of BEAR FLAG REPUBLIC, the respected insider's newsletter on "eating, drinking, sleeping and getting around in California." Their style is relaxed and they write with expertise, honesty and humor. Bob is an advertising executive whose extensive traveling inspired BEAR FLAG. He is a Southern California editor of CALIFORNIA CRITIC and contributor to LOS ANGELES MAGAZINE. Raye had a career in advertising and television before raising two sons and a daughter. Both have an appreciation of good food, good wine, good service and the many intangibles which make a restaurant "tops."

THE TOP TEN RESTAURANTS
OF CALIFORNIA

Picking the top ten restaurants of California is no easy matter. And ranking them borders on the impossible. But pick them and rank them we did . . . after months of examination, conversation, consternation and agitation.

Some were picked for excellence of cuisine and service. Others for bringing excitement to dining. And some for serving fine, imaginative food at fair prices most diners can afford.

Each deserves to be recognized for making a meaningful contribution to the California dining experience.

TOP TEN RESTAURANTS OF CALIFORNIA

L'ORANGERIE   **(415) 776-3600**
419 O'Farrell St.
  (between Taylor and Jones)
Downtown San Francisco

A great restaurant is a combination of outstanding kitchen and masterfully run dining room, blended in an inviting atmosphere. There's many a restaurant in California with an inviting atmosphere. And a few with outstanding kitchens. But it's close to impossible to find a place where someone really runs the dining room. The classic art of the Maitre d'Hotel is disappearing.

L'Orangerie is #1 in California because it is the one restaurant that has it all. The atmosphere is formal but relaxed... no stuffiness here. The main dining room suggests an orange arbor. The bar a library. Everything is very proper, but also friendly. Every contact from telephone reservation to greeting at the door to parting farewell is handled as though you are an honored guest.

Chef Alphonse Acheritogarary runs a magnificent kitchen. Food is consistently outstanding. L'Orangerie's Quenelles de Poisson a Notre Maniere are superior. Le Coq en Pate (a boneless breast of chicken baked with goose livers and truffles in a flaky pastry shell) is prepared for two — and is one of the finest dishes served in California. The menu features 18 entrees... many unusual. Plus daily specials.

The Maitre d' Hotel is Hans Brandt, and it is a delight to see this master at work. Brandt is not only a fine host who sees that every customer is treated with care, but he also keeps everything in L'Orangerie's dining room under total control at all times. Hans Brandt teams well with Alphonse Acheritogarary to make L'Orangerie tops.

Dinner and After-theater   Reservations Recommended
    Supper: Mon.-Sat.   Major Cards
Price: Expensive   Valet Parking
Full Bar   Dress: Jackets

L'ORANGERIE

QUENELLES DE POISSON A NOTRE MANIERE . 3.75
a fish mousse, with a clam sauce,
our specialty served as a main course . . 8.00

SAUMON POCHE SAUCE MOUSSELINE
ou
SAUMON GRILLE 9.50

TURBOT POCHE SAUCE HOLLANDAISE . . 10.50
imported french turbot when available

SOLE DU PAS-DE-CALAIS MEUNIERE . . 9.75
imported french sole

CANARD A L'ORANGERIE . . . . for two 20.50
at least 35 minutes

FAISAN EN SALMIS PERIGOURDINE . for two 24.00
pheasant & goose liver

LE COQ EN PATE . . . . . for two 21.50
our specialty, with goose liver and truffles; 25 minutes

FILET DE PORC EN CHEVREUIL . . . 9.50
in a game sauce, when available

CARRE DE PORC A L'ORANGERIE . . . 7.50
our pork specialty, with orange and cognac

MEDAILLON DE VEAU MEDERIC . . . 10.25
cream and mushrooms

NOISETTE DE VEAU "LUR-SALUCES" . . 10.25
flown in, milk fed veal, our creation

POULET ROTI CRESSONNIERE . . . (for two) 17.00

ENTRECOTE BORDELAISE OU FINES HERBES . . 11.75
favorite french beef cut

STEACK AU POIVRE CHEF ALPHONSE . . 12.25
with pepper, cream and cognac

TOURNEDOS ROSSINI 12.25

TOP TEN RESTAURANTS OF CALIFORNIA

SCANDIA   **(213) 278-3555**
9040 Sunset Blvd.
   (near Doheny)
Sunset Strip, Los Angeles

Scandia is L.A.'s best restaurant . . . and one of the best big restaurants anywhere. The food is consistently excellent, variety enormous, service attentive, the wine list superior, and the cocktails are large, mixed with care and handsomely presented. But Scandia is even more. It is a festive restaurant . . . a place to celebrate good times. And it is a great value (there are still two dinner entrees under $5, ten under $8). It is easy to run up a healthy tab, however, as Scandia's appetizers and desserts border on the irresistible.

The menu is long and diverse. Seafood and the daily specials are especially recommended. Scandia's only problem is that it is too popular, and you must call days ahead to reserve a table during popular dining hours. Founder/owner Ken Hansen has built a remarkable restaurant. So good, it's worth adjusting your dining timetable. What's more, if you're a late diner, you can also select from a "bargain" supper menu. Or enjoy Scandia at lunch or for a superior Sunday brunch.

Dinner: Tues.-Sun.   Reservations Vital
Lunch: Tues.-Sat.   (and call several days
Brunch: Sun., 11-2:30   ahead)
Supper: Tues.-Sun., 10:30-   Cards: CB, MC, V(BA)
   Midnight   Jackets Required
Price: Moderate to Expensive
Full Bar

Scandia

APPETIZERS THE HOT DELIGHTS

The Mushrooms with Deviled Crab . . . . ·3.50
Crabmeat cooked with shallots and mustard and stuffed in mushroom caps.

Viking Plättar 3.50
Miniature pancakes flavored with aquavit and served with sour cream and Danish caviar.

The Coquille 4.50
Small Norwegian lobster tails, white wine sauce with grapes.

The Crepe 3.75
Thin pancake wrapped around tiny coral-pink Shrimps in Dill and Hollandaise, glaced under fire.

The Great Hamlets Dagger 4.50
Tiny lobster tails deviled and broiled on the skewer, served with an ice-cold sauce made with caviar and aquavit.

―SCANDIA SPECIALTIES―

Kalvfilet Oskar 9.85
Veal cutlet saute, garnished with asparagus tips, crablegs, sauce bearnaise.

Böf Med Lög 9.25
Tenderloin steak with onions fried in butter.

Biff Lindström 4.85
Chopped steak mixed with chopped beets, onions and capers, topped with fried egg.

Källdolmar 4.75
The tender leaves of white cabbage filled with a veal and pork stuffing with rice. Braised in the Swedish manner and served with cucumber salad and Lingon.

Spring Chicken Saute, Louise 5.50
Unjointed, sauteed in butter with shallots and fresh mushrooms, finished with fresh cream and a dash of old sherry.

Tournedos Theodora 10.50
Two small filet mignons garnished with gooseliver, bouquets of vegetables, sauce madeira.

Lammesaddel *for 2 or more* per person 10.50
Young filet of lamb, roasted and prepared in the Scandia way, carved and served at your table.

"Viking Sword" *(Served for no less than 2 persons)* per person . . . 12.50
Large brochette of broiled breast of turkey, small Chateau-Briand, center of a smoked pork chop, tomatoes and mushrooms, served on a flaming sword with many kinds of vegetables and sauce bearnaise.

FISH AND SHELLFISH

Danish Dover Sole, *Specialty of the House* 9.75
Cooked in chablis, stuffed with coral pink shrimps in lobster sauce, glaced with white wine sauce.

Danish Plaice 6.50
The flounder of the North Sea sauteed in butter, Sauce Remoulade a part.

The Trout 8.25
Filets of the rainbow sauteed with tiny lobster tails and peeled grapes.

The Virgin-Lobster Tails 7.75
Tiny Norwegian lobster tails breaded in fresh crumbs and fried with fresh parsley and sauce remoulade.

Broiled Fresh Lake Superior Whitefish (Boned) 7.75
With Cucumbers in Sour Cream.

Poached Danish Turbot *with Horseradish Hollandaise* 9.50

Planked Fresh Whitefish — or Salmon for 2 . . . . . . 18.50
Served for 2 or more Only

Imported Dover Sole, Saute or Broiled 9.50

TOP TEN RESTAURANTS OF CALIFORNIA

(#3)

RISTORANTE ORSI   **(415) 981-6535**
375 Bush St.
(Between Kearny and Montgomery)
Financial District, San Francisco

Being the best Italian restaurant in San Francisco is indeed an achievement...and that honor has been earned by Orsi. The two owners are Chef Oreste Orsi and Joseph Orsini, who looks after the dining rooms. Both are usually present. Food is Northern Italian. Pasta homemade, prepared al dente and sauced almost any way you want it. Fish and veal dishes are outstanding. Fine wine list. Excellent bar.

At dinner, Orsi's features both a la carte and complete dinner menus. The more adventurous features are a la carte, however the dinner is a terrific value for the hungry (salad, crab or oysters a la "Orsi," tortellini, choice of 26 entrees, dessert and coffee for $10.75 to $15 depending on your entree).

Orsi's can be a bit hectic during the lunch rush, but takes on a quiet dignity during the dinner hour.

Dinner: Mon.-Sat.	Reservations Recommended
Lunch: Mon.-Fri.	Major Cards
Price: Moderate to Expensive	Valet Parking
Full Bar	Dress: Jackets

Orsi's

TOSSED GREEN SALAD
CRAB OR OYSTERS A LA "ORSI"
TORTELLINI

FILET OF PETRALE 10.75
PETRALE, CALTOCCIO 11.00
ABALONE STEAK 14.75
FROG LEGS ALLA "ORSI" 10.75
BROILED CHICKEN 10.75
CHICKEN CACCIATORE 11.00
CHICKEN PAESANA 11.00
BREAST OF CAPON ALLA "ORSI" 11.25
SCAMPI MUGNAIA 14.50

SCALOPPINE, MUSHROOMS 11.50

SCALOPPINE ALLA "ORSI" 11.50

SCALOPPINE PICCATA 11.00

SCALOPPINE ALL'AGRO 11.00

VEAL PARMIGIANA 11.50

PAIARDA DI VITELLA 11.00

UCCELLETTI SCAPPATI 11.75

SALTIMBOCCA ALLA FLORENTINE 11.50

BROILED WHOLE SQUAB 13.75

BONED ROYAL SQUAB,
    Cherry Sauce 15.25

BONED ROYAL SQUAB, Florentine 14.75

MEDAGLIONE OF BEEF WITH MUSHROOM .. 14.25

GRENADIN OF BEEF alla "ORSI 14.25

SPIEDINO DI FILETTO (BROCHETTE) 13.50

DOUBLE FRENCH LAMB CHOPS 15.25

NEW YORK CUT SIRLOIN 15.00

FILET MIGNON 15.00

| ICE CREAM | SHERBET | SPUMONI |

BANANA FRITTA   CREMA ALLA FIAMMA

COFFEE

ANTHONY'S FISH GROTTO   (714) 232-5103
ANTHONY'S STAR OF THE
   SEA ROOM   (714) 232-7408
1360 Harbor Drive
   (at Ash St.)
Embarcadero, San Diego

Anthony's is a "something for everyone" restaurant operation that not only works, but works very well. It's a two-restaurant complex that gives you a choice.

1.) Anthony's Fish Grotto is the "people's restaurant." Nothing fancy on the menu...just lots of fish (mostly fresh), simply but marvelously prepared, and served at bargain prices. There are no reservations and waits can be long.

2.) Anthony's Star of the Sea Room is for those who seek a formal, elegant dining experience. Excellent gourmet seafood dishes are prepared with care and served with style. Reservations well in advance are vital.

The two Anthony's share a single building which juts out over San Diego Bay and offers spectacular views of the harbor action. The Ghio family operates other good restaurants in the San Diego area – but the two on the Embarcadero are the super stars!

ANTHONY'S FISH GROTTO

Dinner & Lunch: Wed.-Mon.	No Reservations
Lower Priced to Moderate	Cards: MC, V(BA)
Full Bar	Self Parking

ANTHONY'S STAR OF THE SEA ROOM

Dinner: Every Night	Reservations Vital
Price: Expensive	Cards: MC, V(BA)
Full Bar	Self Parking
	Dress: Jackets and Ties

Other Grottos:

886 Prospect   (714) 454-7135
La Jolla

9530 Murray Drive   (714) 463-0368
La Mesa

"E" Street at Interstate 5   (714) 425-4200
Chula Vista

Star of the Sea Room

Poached Fish a la Embarcadero 7.25
A specially selected fisherman's catch of the day is blended with a little oil and lemon for your discriminating taste, and served with boiled, parsleyed potatoes.

Scallops Bordelaise 7.50
These gourmet morsels from the briny deep take on an even added lustre with Anthony's careful preparation. They are placed in a perfect blend of garlic and parsley and sautéed with the finest sherry.

Cape Cod Scallops 7.50
Sautéed with butter, chives and seasoned bread crumbs.

Deviled Crab 7.50
Spicy and juicy crab legs elegantly served in a giant sea shell.

Coquille "Veronique" 7.50
Tender, succulent Icelandic lobster meat, sautéed in a white lobster sauce, flavored with whole stone peeled grapes.

Frog Legs 7.50
Sautéed in butter then bordelaise sauce to a rare tenderness. Flamed at your table.

Stuffed Filet De Pesca 7.75
Stuffed with select, tiny, tender shrimp and temptingly flavored with a special piquant sauce.

Far Eastern Curry 8.95
This Anthony creation brings far Eastern flavor to our lobster, crab and shrimp; blended with homemade Chutney, shredded coconut, roasted peanuts, chopped chives and grated egg.

Baked Pompano 11.25
From Florida, enhanced with a special sauce from Mrs. Ghio's old world recipes.

Cioppino a la Catherine 11.25
Our own old world fisherman's recipe with "Bib and Tuck."

Lobster Thermidor 19.00
Chunks of California lobster mixed with a wine sauce, cognac and choice mushrooms, then bakes in the original shell.

Sole a l'Admiral (for two) . . . .
A whole petrale sole, stuffed with a most appetizing blend of lobster, shrimp and crab, oven baked, for the gourmet. (Allow 35 min. to prepare)

Anthony's
GROTTO ROOM

ACCLAIMED ENTREES

FISH & CHIPS IN OUR FAMOUS BATTER	3.50
SQUID CUTLETS	2.85
SQUID STEAK	2.95
FRIED SHRIMP	3.35
SCALLOPS, FRIED	3.35
PACIFIC RED SNAPPER, BROILED	2.35
MIXED FRIES FISH & CHIPS SCALLOPS, SHRIMP	3.50

SCALLOPS (Sautéed) BORDELAISE	2.85
ANTHONY'S FRIED LOBSTER	3.95
CRAB CLAWS, FRIED	3.95
FROG LEGS	4.25
SHELL FISH FRIES	5.95
PRAWNS INTERNATIONAL	7.25
ABALONE STEAK	

SEE SEASONAL SPECIALTIES FOR ADDITIONAL ENTREES

SHELL FISH CASSEROLE A LA CATHERINE Mrs. Ghio's Finest with Lobster Meat, Crab Legs and Scallops **5.95**

SALADS

	PACIFIC	GULF
SUPREME, REGULAR	3.10	4.55
SUPREME, SMALL	2.40	3.05
SHRIMP, LOUIE	3.40	4.95
SHRIMP, LOUIE, SMALL Louie Dressing	2.75	3.35
AVOCADO-SHRIMP	2.75	3.35

LOBSTER
SUPREME, REGULAR	5.85
SUPREME, SMALL	3.95
LOBSTER, LOUIE	6.50
LOBSTER, LOUIE, SMALL Louie Dressing	4.35
AVOCADO-LOBSTER	4.35

ALL SUPREME SALADS WITH ANTHONY'S DRESSING

TUNA SALAD (cheese) 2.45
AVOCADO TUNA 2.60

SUPREME, REGULAR	4.50
SUPREME, SMALL	3.15
CRAB, LOUIE	4.90
CRAB, LOUIE, SMALL Louie Dressing	3.60
AVOCADO-CRAB	3.60

COMBINATIONS
SUPREME, REGULAR	4.95
SUPREME, SMALL	3.40
COMB, LOUIE	5.50
COMB, LOUIE, SMALL Louie Dressing	3.65
AVOCADO-COMBINATION	3.65

15

L'ERMITAGE   (213) 652-5840
730 N. La Cienega Blvd.
(No. of Melrose)
Los Angeles

L'Ermitage is a totally elegant restaurant. From decor to table settings to food presentation, elegance abounds. L'Ermitage is also a very good restaurant...emerging as the best French restaurant in Los Angeles. L'Ermitage stands out. A cool, suave atmosphere to enjoy a special dinner or lunch.

Owner-chef Jean Bertranou has studded the menu with many unusual dishes: boneless breast of duckling in Medoc wine, veal chop with puree of onions, mushrooms and sauce Mornay, boneless chicken with sour and sweet sauce. Fish dishes are outstanding. And there is a long list of intriguing hors d'oeuvres. For dessert, L'Ermitage's Souffle Au Grand Marnier is supreme. Extensive wine list.

Dinner: Mon.-Sat.	Reservations Vital
Lunch: Mon.-Fri.	Major Cards
Price: Expensive to Very	Valet Parking
Full Bar	Jacket and Tie at Dinner

L'ERMITAGE

ENTRÉES

SUPREMES DE POULARDE ETUVES AU CHAMPAGNE 10.00
Breast of Capon with Champagne Sauce

PAUPIETTE DE VOLAILLE GRAND VENEUR 10.00
Boneless Chicken Thigh with Sour and Sweet Sauce

AIGUILLETTE DE CANARD AU MEDOC 11.00
Breast of Fresh Duckling Medoc Wine

PIGEON CARPINTERIA GASCONNE 10.00
Boneless Pigeon with Wild Mushrooms

MEDAILLON DE VEAU NORMANDE 14.00
Veal Loin Sauteed with Fresh Apples

COTE DE VEAU PRINCE ORLOFF 14.00
Veal Chop with Puree of Onions, Mushrooms and Sauce Mornay

NOISETTE D'AGNEAU MASSENA 13.00
Loin of Lamb with Madeira Sauce on Artichoke Bottom

PAVÉ DE BOEUF SAUCE MOUTARDE AUX HERBES 13.00
Filet Mignon with Mustard and Herbs

ENTRECOTE A LA MOELLE AU FLEURIE 13.00
Sirloin Steak with Sauce Bordelaise and Marrow

POISSONS

SUPREME DE WHITE FISH BRAISE AUX PETITS LEGUMES 9.50
Filet of White Fish with Julienne Vegetables

FILET DE TRUITE POLATZOFF 9.50
Trout with Mousseline of White Fish and Chives

SOLE DE LA MANCHE BAGATELLE 11.00
Breaded Dover Sole Horseradish Bearnaise Sauce

TRUITE AU BLEU AUX DEUX BEURRES 12.00
Live Trout with Two Butters

TRUITE DES LACS AU BEURRE NANTAIS 9.50
Filet of Lake Trout Muscadet Butter

CROUSTADE DE HOMARD DU MAINE L'ERMITAGE 14.00
Maine Lobster in Pastry Shell Mushrooms, Mussels, and Oysters

CAFE .75   EXPRESSO 1.25   TEA .50

CAPPUCINO 2.50

INFUSIONS .50

VALENTINO   **(213) 829-4313**
3115 Pico Blvd.
   (West of Bundy)
Santa Monica

Los Angeles enjoys an abundance of good Italian restaurants — and at the top is Valentino. It's a young restaurant, still experimenting, still trying new things, which is part of the restaurant's great attraction...the opportunity to try unusual Italian dishes and wine.

Valentino is the creation of Piero Selvaggio, a young restaurateur of the "old school." Piero is not only a charmer with an incredible memory for names and faces, he is a man who understands the makings of fine restaurants: outstanding food plus a style of atmosphere and service which makes customers feel wanted.

Valentino's menu is lengthy and varied, but if you can't find what your heart's set on, tell them what you like...chances are you'll get it. Excellent fish, veal and pasta. And for openers, try the tasty, crisp calamari.

Wine is big at Valentino. Not only do they have one of the best selections in California, but they use the inventory to adorn the walls of two of the dining rooms.

Dinner: Every Night   Reservations Vital
Lunch: Friday Only   Major Cards
Price: Expensive   Valet Parking
Full Bar

Valentino

Pasta e Farinacei

Spaghetti alla Carbonara	5.95
(Bacon, egg, wine, cream)	
Canelloni Rossini	5.95
Penne alla Siciliana	6.25
with Eggplant, Sausages, Tomato	
Lasagne Pasticciate	5.95
...still made by my mother!	
Linguine alle Vongole (Clams)	6.25
Cappellacci alla Trasteverina	5.95
Stuffed with ricotta e spinach	
Fettuccine San Daniele	6.25
with prosciutto, porcini mushrooms, cream	

Vitello ~ Veal

Scaloppine a piacere (any style you like)	8.50
Cotolette a piacere	8.50
Lombata con salsiccia	9.95
veal chop & sausage	
Rosette di Vitella Medallions of Veal	11.50
Paillard di Vitella	10.50

Pollo ~ Chicken

Pollo alla diavola	7.50
Broil, deviled Chicken	
Pollo alla romana, artichokes	7.25
Petto di Pollo Valentino	7.50
stuffed breast of Chicken	
Chicken Peperonata con Salsiccia	7.95
Chicken Portofino	7.50
with pine-nuts & garlic	

TOP TEN RESTAURANTS OF CALIFORNIA

#7

TADICH GRILL   **(415) 391-2373**
240 California St.
(at Front)
Financial District, San Francisco

Tadich is a California institution. It was founded in 1849. And has been run by the Buich family since 1918. It's a plain restaurant. Takes no reservations. To eat dinner requires elbowing your way through the crowd at the bar, catching the attention of the bartender so you can give him your name, then often waiting an hour or more. And when you pay, you need cash. No credit cards or checks here.

So what makes Tadich a Top Restaurant?

It's the food. And the value. And the never ending festive atmosphere. (Tadich is the antithesis of the dignified, formal French restaurant...and everybody loves it). Tadich's steaks are marvelous. And the seafood is San Francisco's best. Portions are large and everything is at "good deal" prices. (When we checked recently, 3 entrees were under $3, 23 were under $5 and 39 under $6). Tadich's menu is printed every day and includes over 60 entrees and 15 large salads, plus dinner salads, appetizers, desserts, etc. At Tadich you can have as much or as little as you like...and almost anything you like.

A Tadich plus...in addition to tables and private booths, Tadich also has counter service, which makes it a great place for the single diner.

Dinner & Lunch: Mon.-Sat.	No Reservations
(closes at 8:30)	No Credit Cards
Price: Moderate	Self Parking
Full Bar	

Tadich Grill

THE ORIGINAL COLD DAY RESTAURANT

1849   OUR 128th YEAR

SMALL SALADS

Served without Entrée 50¢ Extra

Fresh Crab or Prawn 4.15; Shrimp 3.30; Mixed Green 1.30
Heart of Lettuce or Romaine 1.70; . . with Anchovies . 2.30
Small Vegetable Combination . 1.80; . . with Seafood . 3.70
Sliced Tomato Salad with Crab or Shrimp 4.15
Sliced Tomato Salad . 1.70   Half Avocado, French . 1.95
Mixed Seafood Salad . 4.15   Lettuce and Tomato . 1.95
TADICH SPECIAL DINNER SALAD 1.45

FROM THE CHARCOAL BROILER

Top Sirloin Steak with Fresh Mushroom Sauce 7.75
New York Cut Steak, Shoestring Potatoes 7.95
Filet Tips with Fresh Mushroom Sauce 3.25
Filet Mignon with Fresh Mushroom Sauce 8.25
Half Spring Chicken, Shoestring Potatoes. 4.65
Double Lamb Chops . . 6.25   Skirt Steak 4.95
Pork Chops with Applesauce 4.95

FISH — SHELLFISH

All fresh Seafood subject to season, weather and fishing conditions

CHARCOAL BROILED	Fresh Water Baby Salmon	6.40
	Broiled Lobster Tail with Butter Sauce	11.50
	Petrale, Butter Sauce	6.10
	Halibut Steak, Butter Sauce	6.25
	Sea Bass, Butter Sauce	6.25
	Salmon Steak, Butter Sauce	7.75
	Rex Sole or Sandabs, Butter Sauce	5.75
	Fresh Brook Trout Meunière	5.50
BAKED, EN CASSEROLE	Oyster Rockefeller	6.10
	Baked Halibut Florentine, en Casserole	5.25
	Sea Bass, Rice, Créole Sauce	4.50
	Sea Bass and Crab Meat, Créole Sauce	5.25
	Salmon and Shrimps with Rice à la Créole . . .	5.50
	Shrimp Curry and Rice	5.50
	Shrimp and Oyster Créole	5.75
	Stuffed Turbot with Crab & Shrimp à la Newburg	6.75
	Salmon and Crab à la Newburg	6.75
	Deviled Crab	6.75
	Crab Meat and Prawns à la Monza	6.75
	Combination Crab Meat & Lobster Thermidor . .	8.75
STEAMED	Kippered Alaska Cod, Butter Sce., Boiled Potato	4.65
	Smoked Finnan Haddie, Butter, Boiled Potato .	5.25
PAN FRIED	Hangtown Fry (Oyster, Bacon and Eggs) . . .	5.75
	Filet of English Sole, Tartar Sauce	5.25
	Filet of Rock Cod with Sauté Crab or Shrimp .	5.25
	Filet of Rock Cod, Tartar Sauce	4.75
	Filet of Petrale, Tartar Sauce	6.10
	Rex Sole or Sandabs	5.75
	Abalone Steak, Tartar Sauce	8.95
DEEP FRIED	Eastern Oysters with Bacon	6.10
	Scallops, Tartar Sauce	5.95
	Jumbo Prawns, Tartar Sauce	6.75
	Crab Legs, Tartar Sauce	7.95
SAUTÉ	Crab Legs Sauté, Fresh Mushrooms, Sherry Wine	8.25
	Prawns Sauté, Fresh Mushrooms, Sauterne Wine	8.25
	Scallops Sauté, Fresh Mushrooms, Sauterne Wine	7.25

THE SARDINE FACTORY   (408) 373-3775
701 Wave St.
Cannery Row
Monterey

This big, bustling, bountiful restaurant exudes an atmosphere of excitement which makes diners feel good and well rewarded after a marathon meal. Complete dinners include: 1) an antipasto with marinated artichoke hearts, salami, garbanzo and kidney beans and Monterey Jack cheese, 2) abalone cream soup, 3) tossed green salad, 4) hot cheese bread and 5) a choice of well prepared and often original entrees — featuring fine local seafood. Fresh sandabs, salmon, calamari, sole and Dungeness crab, in season. Veal dishes are also recommended. As is the homemade cannoli for dessert.

The restaurant, which sits on the side of a hill overlooking Cannery Row, is a near-museum of Monterey's sardine fishing days, with nostalgic pictures and memorabilia at every turn. The building itself was originally a cantina for cannery employees...but in its history was also a union hall and boxing gym.

Bert Cutino and Ted Balestreri opened the Sardine Factory just ten years ago, and during that time it has evolved into a restaurant of distinction and spirit.

Dinner: Every Night	Reservations Vital
Lunch: Mon.-Sat.	(Reserve for weekends
Price: Moderate to Expensive	in advance)
Full Bar	Major Cards
	Valet Parking

THE SARDINE FACTORY

COMPLETE DINNERS

Special Antipasto Plate, Abalone Cream Soup or Soup du Jour, tossed green salad with our own special choice of dressings, hot cheese bread.

CRAB ALLANDO
The delicate flavor of Pacific Crabmeat combined with Tender Noodles, laced with a Creamy Light Sauce, with a Touch of Tomato and Fine Herbs
7.95

FETTUCCINE CON VONGOLE
Tender Noodles with Fresh Cherrystone Clams and seasoned with Butter, Garlic, Parsley and Fresh Grated Parmigiana and Romano Cheeses
7.95

*SOLE VANESSI
Rolled Fillet of Sole stuffed with Cheese, Crabmeat and Fine Herbs, baked in a Rich Sauce with Shrimp
8.50

*COQUILLES ST. JACQUES
(flown in fresh)
Choice Eastern Scallops in our Own Special Bechamel Sauce with Sherry Wine and Fresh Mushrooms
9.50

PRAWNS ST. JAMES
Choice Crabmeat with Fine Herbs served on Butterfly Shrimp, baked in Hollandaise Sauce. Fresh Spinach Garni
10.95

LOBSTER WELLINGTON
We created this version of the famous dish named after the Duke of Wellington. Tender Lobster Tail, baked in Light Pastry and served with Special Sauce
12.95

CANNELLONI ALLA PASSETTO
A Rolled Crepe with fine seasoned Veal and Fresh Spinach Filling, baked in our Own Special Sauce
7.50

CHICKEN BALTINO
Breast of Capon sautéed with Fresh Mushrooms, Shallots, Fine Herbs, Sauce Tarragon
7.95

VEAL FRANCESCA
Sautéed, Lightly Breaded White Veal, baked in Parmesan Sauce with Ham. Topped with Asparagus Spears and Fontina Cheese
10.95

TOURNEDOS REGINA
The Queen of Meats
Petite Filet Mignon sautéed in Mushroom Sauce with Chives and garnished with Fresh Eggplant and Asparagus Spears
11.95

VEAL CARDINAL
The Sardine Factory's own created dish of thin slices of White Veal and tender Lobster, combined in a Lemon Sauce Extraordinaire.
13.95

FISH & SHELLFISH

CALAMARI
Local Squid, breaded, sautéed in Lemon Butter
7.50

*SANDABS
Monterey's own, caught daily, sautéed Meuniére
8.50

*SOLE
Fresh local Rex Sole, sautéed in Lemon Butter
8.50

*SALMON
Monterey King, served fresh only, grilled or broiled
9.50

ABALONE
Center Cut only, Butter Breaded
12.50

SCAMPI LANGOUSTINE
Baby Lobster Tails sautéed in Wine and Butter Sauce
12.50

LOBSTER TAILS
Two King Size, Tender Australian Lobster Tails, pan broiled
15.95

'FLAMING SARDINE'
A unique combination of Coffee and Liqueur Flambe' at your table.
2.50

23

BERNARD'S   **(213) 624-0183**
Biltmore Hotel
515 So. Olive St.
   (between 5th and 6th)
Downtown Los Angeles

Bernard's is the wonderful new restaurant in Los Angeles' venerable old Biltmore Hotel. The hotel changed hands recently and new architect/owners Phyllis Lambert and Gene Summers have spent millions transforming the Biltmore into a modern day showplace. One of their moves was to invest in a fine restaurant.

The result is Bernard's which, under the guidance of Bernard Jacoupy, has quickly and decisively established itself as one of California's best restaurants. Decor blends Mies van der Rohe furniture and Rococo ceilings in a handsome tiered room studded with living potted trees. Service is knowledgable and precise. Food is French — with an emphasis on fish and seafood. Sauces are marvelous. And care is taken to skillfully prepare each dish.

Bernard's is a fine special occasion restaurant in the heart of Downtown Los Angeles.

Dinner: Mon.-Sat.   Reservations Recommended
Lunch: Mon.-Fri.   Major Cards
Price: Expensive to Very   Valet Parking
Full Bar   at Olive St. Entrance
                           Dress: Jackets

Les Poissons et Crustaces Frais

Le Red Snapper au Champagne   *9.00*

Poached Red Snapper Fillet with Champagne Sauce

Les Paupiettes de Sole Argenteuil   *10.00*

*Poached Fillet of Sole Served with a
White Wine Sauce and Asparagus Tips*

Le Filet de Sanddab aux Tomates et Courgettes   *8.50*

*Sanddabs Sauteed with Fresh Tomatoes and
Zucchini*

La Lotte Rotie au Cidre   *8.50*

Fillet of Lote Roasted in Apple Cider

Le Whitefish a la Moutarde de Meaux   *8.50*

Whitefish with a Mustarde de Meaux Sauce

Le Homard Grille Beurre Blanc   **According to Weight**

Broiled Lobster with White Butter Sauce

Les Poissons et Crustaces Importes

La Quenelle de Brochet Nantua   *8.00*

Quenelle of Pike Cooked in a Lobster Sauce

La Darne de Saumon au Poivre Vert   *9.00*

*Poached Salmon Steak with a Green Peppercorn
Veloute Sauce*

Les Viandes

Le Grenadin de Veau Normande   *10.00*

*Medallions of Veal Sauteed and Served with
Fresh Apples*

L'Entrecote de Boeuf Sauce Bordelaise   *12.50*

Broiled New York Cut Served with Bordelaise Sauce

Le Tournedos Bernard   *13.50*

Filet Mignon Bernard's, Truffle Sauce

MAMA'S

Union Square, Nob Hill, Washington Square:
San Francisco; Also San Mateo

Mama's makes the "Top Ten" list because it does what it does better than anyone else. Mama's is a superb "fast food" restaurant.

Mama's started as a tiny, modified-cafeteria-style restaurant on Washington Square. We prefer two newer versions where Mama's art has been perfected: in the Cellar in Macy's Department Store on Union Square, and Grovesnor Tower Apartments atop Nob Hill. They differ in style (Macy's is buffet, Nob Hill, full service), but both feature the essentials that make Mama's tops. Fresh fruit, crab, shrimp, tuna, cheeses, eggs, meats, chicken and delicious breads and rolls transformed into marvelous sandwiches, salads and M'omelettes. Also tempting desserts, lots of juices, wines and beer.

Frances and Michael Sanchez (Mama and Papa) have created a California menu and geared it to serving imaginative, quality food quickly. And at good deal prices. Mama's sets a new standard for "gourmet fast food."

Macy's, Union Square   **(415) 391-3790**
San Francisco
Dinner, Lunch, Breakfast: No Reservations
  Mon.-Fri., 9:30 AM-   Cards: Macy's Chg., AE
  7:30 PM (Sat., 5 PM)   Self Parking
Lower Priced to Moderate
Wine and Beer

Grovesnor Tower Apts.   **(415) 928-1004**
1177 California St.
Nob Hill, San Francisco
Dinner, Lunch, Breakfast: Reservations Accepted
  Daily   Cards: MC, V(BA)
Price: Moderate   Validated Parking in Garage
Full Bar

Original Mama's   **(415) 362-6421**
1701 Stockton St.
Washington Sq., San Francisco

Macy's, Hillsdale   **(415) 573-1176**
  Shopping Center
San Mateo

Mama's

Salads & Cold Plates

NOB HILL SALAD
Breast of chicken, fresh fruit and
avocado with our own fruit dressing.
6.50

PAPA'S FAVORITE
Dungeness crab meat and fresh
fruit with sliced tomatoes.
6.25

SYL'S SUMMER SALAD
Garden greens, tomatoes,
cucumbers, ham and cheese.
4.25

COLD PLATE
Roast Beef, Baked Ham, Salami,
and assorted cheeses with
tossed green salad or cole slaw.
4.65

CRAB LOUIE
6.95
SHRIMP LOUIE
5.25

BILL and JOANNA'S SALAD
Dungeness crab meat, carrot-raisin
salad, and our own crisp cole slaw
with sliced tomatoes and cucumbers.
6.25

TUNA SALAD
Chunks of Albacore tuna with
baby white potatoes,
string beans and tomatoes.
5.75

FRESH FRUIT
with cottage cheese or yogurt.
4.25

Veal Specialties

VEAL DORÉ **7.25**
Thin slices of veal sauté
in lemon and butter sauce.

VEAL MARSALA **7.25**
Choice veal and fresh mushrooms
simmered in the full-flavored,
sweet wine of Marsala.

BABY WHITE VEAL **9.95**
In our chef's special sauce

VEAL A LA PARMIGIANA **7.35**

VEAL SCOLLOPINE **7.35**

VEAL TOSCANA **7.35**
Thinly sliced veal sauteed with
fresh mushrooms and onion in a
blend of white wine and pale dry
sherry with mild Italian peppers.

VEAL SAUTÉ **6.85**

Meat & Poultry

CHICKEN SALVATORE **6.95**
Boneless breast of chicken sauté
with prosciutto, cheese, and fresh
mushrooms.

ROASTED CHICKEN **6.25**

NEW YORK STEAK **9.50**

JOE'S SPECIAL **5.75**

FILET OF BEEF A LA MARSALA **7.95**
Tender medallions of beef and
whole fresh mushrooms sauteed
in a blend of three fine
wines and delicate spices.

BARBAGELATA SPECIAL **4.95**
Mama's ground chuck steak, sauteed
golden mushrooms and fresh zucchini.

PRIME RIB (Saturday only) **8.25**

All entrees served with fresh vegetables, sauteed potatoes
or pasta and our own baguette bread.

M'Omelettes

golden eggs cooked in butter with toasted Baguette and orange slices

Fresh Mushroom and Parsley **3.95**   Cheese **3.45**   Ham and Cheese **3.95**

Green Chili and Sour Cream **3.95**   Spanish **3.95**   Spinach & Sour Cream **3.95**

Fresh Fruit and Sour Cream **3.95**   Chicken Liver and Bacon **4.25**

THE UNION SQUARE **4.15**
Bacon & Fontina cheese

SAN FRANCISCO EXPERIENCE **5.25**
Dungeness crab & Secrets

MAMA'S CHILDREN'S FAVORITE
Mushrooms, sauteed green onions, grilled tomatoes and jack cheese
4.15

TOP TEN RESTAURANTS OF
LOS ANGELES/ORANGE COUNTIES

BERNARD'S   **(213) 624-0183**
Biltmore Hotel
515 S. Olive Street
  (between 5th and 6th)
Downtown Los Angeles

See "Top Ten Restaurants of California," pages 24-25.

LE CELLIER   **(213) 828-1585**
2628 Wilshire Blvd.
  (at Princeton)
Santa Monica

Le Cellier has lots going for it: consistency in the kitchen, daily specials, unusual monthly or seasonal dishes, careful service and dignified atmosphere...all at prices which make it one of L.A.'s better lunch and dinner values. Owners are Jacques and Madeleine Don-Salat who host and Chef Jean Bellorde who runs the kitchen. Complete dinners include soup and salad.

Dinner: Tues.-Sun.   Reservations Vital
Lunch: Tues.-Fri.   Major Cards
Price: Moderate to Expensive   Valet Parking
Full Bar

CHANTECLAIR   **(714) 752-8001**
18912 MacArthur Blvd.
  (West of San Diego Fwy.)
Irvine

Beautiful restaurant in the style of a French country inn serves well prepared and handsomely presented dishes. Gourmet seafood, veal, beef menu. Elaborate, expensive, special occasion Sunday lunch. Outstanding cocktail lounge.

Dinner: Every Night   Reservations Advised
Lunch: Mon.-Fri.   Major Cards
Price: Expensive   Parking Lot
Full Bar   Dress: Lunch, Casual;
                                      Dinner, Jackets

CHEZ CARY   (714) 542-3595
571 So. Main St.
Orange

You're treated like royalty in this posh, intensive-service restaurant — addressed by name, seated in ornate velvet chairs (with foot stools, if you wish), pampered as you dine, and even met by your car waiting at the door, as you depart. The Continental menu features a varied selection of well prepared entrees, plus some excellent appetizers.

Dinner: Every Night   Reservations a Must
Price: Expensive to Very   Major Cards
Full Bar   Valet Parking
                            Dress: Jackets and Ties

L'ERMITAGE   (213) 652-5840
730 N. La Cienega Blvd.
  (No. of Melrose)
Los Angeles

See "Top Ten Restaurants of California," pages 16-17.

L'ESCOFFIER   (213) 274-7777
Beverly Hilton Hotel
9876 Wilshire Blvd.
  (at Santa Monica)
Beverly Hills

L'Escoffier is created for special occasion dining—a formal, glass-walled room atop the *Beverly Hilton* with a view of the city at night. Beautiful table settings, gracious service, music and dancing (intelligently handled so it does not intrude on the dinner). Elegant food, and a parting rose for each lady. Two complete dinners are featured, *Le Menu Classique* and the fancier *Le Diner Escoffier*. You can also order a la carte from the French Continental menu.

Dinner: Mon.-Sat.   Reservations a Must
Price: Expensive to Very   Major Cards
Full Bar/Dancing   Valet and Self Parking
                            Dress: Jackets

PAPADAKIS TAVERNA   (213) 548-1186
301 W. 6th St.
  (East of Gaffey)
San Pedro

Owner John Papadakis serves up an evening of total enjoyment in this happy, attractive Greek restaurant where both customers and employees have a good time. The well prepared Greek food is accompanied by outbursts of Greek music and athletic folk dancing by John and his waiters. The menu lists traditional favorites such as stuffed grape leaves, Mousaka, Pastistio (Greek lasagna) and roast lamb. Papadakis' wine list is good, and prices very fair. It's a terrific evening for the *whole* family.

Dinner: Tues.-Sun.	Reservations Vital
Price: Moderate	Cards: MC, V(BA)
Wine and Beer	Parking Lot Across Street

SCANDIA   (213) 278-3555
9040 Sunset Blvd.
  (near Doheny)
Sunset Strip, West Hollywood

See "Top Ten Restaurants of California," Pages 10-11.

THE SEASHELL   (213) 884-6500
19723 Ventura Blvd.
  (West of Corbin)
Tarzana
This young restaurant has quickly established itself by not only serving some of the finest seafood in Los Angeles, but also by featuring dishes rarely seen in the city. Fresh local and flown-in Eastern seafood is complemented by select frozen product (they'll tell you which) so well handled, you'd swear it was fresh (Seashell's marvelous abalone, for example). Well operated by Dieter Wantig, out front, and Chef Christian Desmet.

Dinner: Every Night	Reservations Recommended
Lunch: Mon.-Fri.	Major Cards
Price: Moderate to Expensive	Street Parking
Full Bar	

VALENTINO   (213) 829-4313
3115 Pico Blvd.
  (West of Bundy)
Santa Monica
See "Top Ten Restaurants of California," Pages 18-19.

TOP TEN FRENCH RESTAURANTS OF LOS ANGELES/ORANGE COUNTIES

BERNARD'S   **(213) 624-1083**
Biltmore Hotel
5th and Olive Streets
Downtown Los Angeles

See "Top Ten Restaurants of California," Pages 24-25.

LE CELLIER   **(213) 828-1585**
2628 Wilshire Blvd.
  (at Princeton)
Santa Monica

See "Top Ten Restaurants of Los Angeles/Orange Counties,"
  Page 28.

L'ERMITAGE   **(213) 652-5840**
730 N. La Cienega Blvd.
  (No. of Melrose)
Los Angeles

See "Top Ten Restaurants of California," Pages 16-17.

MA MAISON   **(213) 655-1991**
8368 Melrose Ave.
  (East of La Cienega)
Los Angeles
    Chef Wolfgang Puck makes Ma Maison a contender for
the "Best French Food in Los Angeles" award. Owner Patrick
Terrail, who watches over the dining room, is a La Tour
d'Argent Terrail who traded Paris for Los Angeles. The restaurant is an old two-story house with the most comfortable
seating downstairs.

Dinner & Lunch: Mon.-Sat.	Reservations Vital
Price: Expensive to Very	Major Cards
Full Bar	Valet Parking
	Jackets Preferred at Dinner

31

CAFE PARISIEN   (213) 822-2020
3100 Washington Blvd.
  (West of Lincoln)
Marina del Rey

This friendly little restaurant is one of the better places to eat in the Marina. Food is good. Service personal and concerned. Owners Odette and Raymond go out of their way to make you feel welcome. Cafe Parisien is a real "sleeper" for a relaxed dinner in the "hurry-up" Marina.

Dinner: Tues.-Sun.	Reservations Advised
Price: Moderate	Major Cards
Wine and Beer	Parking Lot in Rear

LES PYRENEES   (213) 828-7503
2455 Santa Monica Blvd.
  (West of 26th)
Santa Monica

This handsome, elegant restaurant, although still young, is emerging as one of L.A.'s very best. Food, service and decor all have great appeal. It is a total "make you feel good" effort. Creative dishes such as Sole-Three-Ways and Lamb Wellington. Appetizing presentation of food.

Dinner: Tues.-Sun.	Reservations Recommended
Price: Expensive	Major Cards
Wine and Beer	Self Parking

LE SANGLIER   (213) 345-0470
18760 Ventura Blvd.
  (Facing Crebs Ave.)
Tarzana

Owner Alain Cuny is an inventive chef who likes to get away from standard preparation of French dishes. He adds flavor and flair to regular menu and blackboard specials. Worthy entrees are Cous-Cous on Thursdays, Bouillabaisse every Friday and Quail served Wednesday through Sunday. Soup and salad with entrees.

Dinner: Tues.-Sun.	Reservations Advised
Price: Moderate to Expensive	Major Cards
Full Bar Service	Street Parking

LA SERRE   (213) 990-0500
12969 Ventura Blvd.
(West of Coldwater Canyon)
Studio City

La Serre means "greenhouse" which is the inspiration for the indoor garden setting of this fine restaurant, with its brick floors, white lattice, green walls and abundant ferns. Care and attention go into everything at La Serre — whether it be the decor, food, or even the well-mixed cocktails. One impressive dish is Salad des Fruit de Mer — a salad which draws "ohs" and "ahs" whenever it is served.

Dinner: Mon.-Sat.	Reservations a Must
Lunch: Mon.-Fri.	Cards: AE, MC, V(BA)
Price: Expensive to Very	Valet Parking
Full Bar	

LE ST. TROPEZ   (714) 673-7883
3012 Newport Blvd.
Newport Beach

This attractive little French restaurant puts you in a festive mood the moment you enter — the inviting aroma, professional greeting, dressy dining room. The excellent menu is limited . . . we suggest Medallions de Veau or Mignonettes de Bouef.

Dinner: Tues.-Sun.	Reservations Vital
Price: Moderate to Expensive	Major Cards
Full Bar Service	Parking Lot in Rear
	Dress: Jackets Required

VERONIQUE   (213) 949-7711
8536 Rosemead Blvd.
Pico Rivera

A top French restaurant in a part of town where top restaurants are few and far between. Veronique is comfortable and decorated with taste, but it's the food of owner/chef Georges Mardot which is the attraction.

Dinner: Tues.-Sun.	Reservations Recommended
Lunch: Tues.-Fri.	Major Cards
Price: Moderate	Parking Lot
Wine and Beer	

TOP TEN ITALIAN RESTAURANTS OF
LOS ANGELES/ORANGE COUNTIES

AMELIA'S   **(714) 642-9434**
3300 West Coast Highway
Newport Beach
    One of the prettiest restaurants in Southern California puts the emphasis on seafood Italian-style. The setting is redolent of a Mediterranean country inn — pegged floors, huge fireplace, etched glass, lush plants. A knockout.

Dinner: Every Night	Reservations for Sure
Lunch: Mon.-Fri.	Cards: DC, MC, V(BA)
Price: Moderate to Expensive	Parking Lot
Full Bar	

Original Amelia's   **(714) 673-6580**
311 Marine Ave.
Balboa Island

ANNA MARIA RISTORANTE   **(213) 935-2089**
1356 S. La Brea Ave.
   (South of Olympic)
Midtown Los Angeles
    Savory Neopolitan cooking. Outdoor patio at lunchtime and warm evenings. Try the baked clams . . . and other seafood. Exceptional Italian at fair prices. Daily specials are recommended.

Dinner: Tues.-Sun.	Reservations Recommended
Lunch: Tues.-Fri.	Cards: AE, MC, V(BA)
Lower Priced to Moderate	Parking Lot
Wine and Beer	

Other Location:
418 Wilshire Blvd.   **(213) 395-9285**
   (Between 4th and 5th)
Santa Monica

RISTORANTE CHIANTI   **(213) 653-8333**
7383 Melrose Ave.
   (between La Brea and Fairfax)
Los Angeles
    Ristorante Chianti is chic, popular, expensive and molto

buono. Renowned for over forty years for its superb Northern Italian cooking, Chianti excels with classic veal, chicken and favorite pasta dishes. Carefully selected wine list.

Dinner: Mon.-Sat.	Reservations Vital
Price: Expensive	Cards: AE, MC, V(BA)
Full Bar	Valet Parking

DAN TANA'S   (213) 275-9444
9071 Santa Monica Blvd.
(East of Doheny)
West Hollywood

Dan Tana's is the Los Angeles restaurant most like the restaurants that populate San Francisco's North Beach—crowded, lots of bar action, complete Italian dinners from antipasto to minestrone, to pasta, to entree and coffee. All good.

Dinner: Every Night	Reservations Advised
Price: Moderate to Expensive	Major Cards
Full Bar	Parking Lot

DANTE   (213) 478-3372
11917 Wilshire Blvd.
(West of Barrington)
West Los Angeles

This classy little Italian restaurant is almost hidden among Wilshire Boulevard store fronts, but it is worth seeking out. Food is well prepared, and prices right. Veal, chicken and fish dishes are outstanding.

Dinner: Tues.-Sun.	Reservations Recommended
Lunch: Tues.-Fri.	Parking Lot
Price: Moderate	Cards: DC, MC, V(BA)
Wine and Beer	

LA DOLCE VITA   (213) 278-1845
9785 Santa Monica Blvd.
(just East of Wilshire Crossing)
Beverly Hills

La Dolce Vita has two big attractions: (1) Their Italian food is excellent — actually some of the best prepared veal, fish and pasta dishes in the west. (2) It is a mecca for the show biz set. (One of L.A.'s best places to see and be seen.) Always crowded.

Dinner: Mon.-Sat.	Reservations Vital
Price: Moderate to Expensive	Major Cards
Full Bar	Valet Parking

GINO'S RISTORANTE   (213) 799-8225
5 Pasadena Ave.
South Pasadena

An appetizing array of Italian food—outstanding pasta, veal
and seafood. Dinners with soup, salad and fruit. Try it when
you visit the Norton Simon Museum or Huntington Library.

Dinner: Tues.-Sat.	Reservations a Must
Lunch: Tues.-Fri.	Cards: DC, MC, V(BA)
Price: Moderate	Parking Lot
Wine and Beer	

OROFINO   (213) 880-4622
4505 Las Virgenes Rd.
(Malibu Canyon ¼ mi. West of Ventura Fwy.)
Calabasas

Not much for looks, but unique Italian food, and plenty of
it. Daily specials are often impressive seafood dishes. Imagina-
tion in the kitchen and care up front are displayed by the
Orofino brothers.

Dinner: Every Night	Reservations Suggested
Lunch: Mon.-Fri.	Cards: MC, V(BA)
Brunch: Sat. & Sun., 10-2	Parking Lot
Price: Moderate	
Wine and Beer	

STUFT NOODLE   (714) 548-7418
215 Riverside Drive
(1 block East of Coast Hwy.)
Newport Beach

Warm, Italian, informal. Manicotti, mostaccioli, lasagna,
and eggplant dishes, plus good veal, all at value prices. Dinners
include a tureen of minestrone, salad, garlic bread, cheese and
fruit. Always busy.

Dinner: Tues.-Sun.	Reservations Advised
Lower Priced to Moderate	Cards: AE, MC
Wine and Beer	Parking Lot

VALENTINO   (213) 829-4313
3115 Pico Blvd.
(West of Bundy)
Santa Monica

See "Top Ten Restaurants of California," pages 18-19.

TOP TEN CONTINENTAL RESTAURANTS OF
LOS ANGELES/ORANGE COUNTIES

CHEZ CARY   **(714) 542-3595**
571 So. Main St.
Orange
See "Top Ten Restaurants of Los Angeles/Orange Counties,"
    page 29.

GINGERHOUSE INTERNATIONAL
18669 Ventura Blvd.   **(213) 881-0660**
    (West of Reseda Blvd.)
Tarzana
    Imaginative, rich cooking in a restaurant/art gallery set-
ting. A little of everything including palm reading, but the
inventive menu is the big attraction.

Dinner: Every Night   Reservations Advised
Lunch: Mon.-Fri.   Major Cards
Brunch: Sun., 11-3   Street Parking
Price: Moderate to Expensive
Wine and Beer

HEMINGWAY'S   **(714) 673-9795**
217 Marine Ave.
Balboa Island
    Always fresh, carefully prepared foods are the trademark
of this choice little restaurant. Snapper, bass, yellowtail, salmon
– plus chicken, veal and our favorite pepper steak. Fanciful
desserts.

Dinner: Tues.-Sun.   Reservations for Sure
Lunch: Tues.-Fri.   Cards: CB, MC, V(BA)
Brunch: Sat., Sun. 9-2   Street Parking
Price: Moderate
Wine and Beer

New Additional Location:
2441 West Coast Highway   **(714) 673-0120**
Corona del Mar

MALDONADO'S   (213) 796-1126
1202 E. Green Street
Pasadena

Good continental dinners served with live opera, harp and piano music combine to make Maldonado's one of the Southland's better special occasion restaurants. An all-round good time . . . reasonably priced.

Dinner: Every Night	Reservations a Must
Lunch: Mon.-Fri.	Cards: MC, V(BA)
Price: Moderate to Expensive	Parking Lot
Full Bar plus Music	

POLONAISE   (213) 274-7246
225 So. Beverly Drive
  (South of Wilshire Blvd.)
Beverly Hills

There still are some Polish dishes on the menu, but owner-chef Jean Rouard has directed Polonaise primarily towards French and Basque cooking. And very good too. Seafood is a specialty. Comfortable, appealing atmosphere.

Dinner: Tues.-Sun.	Reservations Recommended
Price: Moderate to Expensive	Major Cards
Full Bar	Valet Parking

SASIAIN'S FOR DINNER   (213) 762-1151
11622 Ventura Blvd.
  (East of Laurel Canyon)
Studio City

Leisurely enjoy a 5-course, fixed-price dinner. A typical menu: (1) antipasto with chilled Cornish game hen, (2) canneloni, (3) trout almondine, (4) filet mignon and poultry topped with mushrooms, accompanied with salad, (5) cheese, fruit and demitasse.

Dinner: Every Night	Reservations Essential
Price: Expensive	Cards: CB, MC, V(BA)
Wine and Beer	Street Parking

SCANDIA   (213) 278-3555
9040 Sunset Blvd.
  (East of Doheny)
Sunset Strip, West Hollywood

See "Top Ten Restaurants of California," Pages 10-11.

THE SILO   (213) 376-7959
900 Manhattan Ave.
Manhattan Beach

    This stylish restaurant is a welcome addition to the beach area. They emphasize fresh seafood. Also duckling, stroganoff and a different veal dish daily. Paella prepared for two, or more, (24-hours notice, please).

Dinner: Tues.-Sun.	Reservations Advised
Brunch: Sun., 10-2:30	Major Cards
Price: Moderate to Expensive	Street Parking
Full Bar	

ST. MORITZ   (213) 980-1122
11720 Ventura Blvd.
  (East of Laurel Canyon)
Studio City

    Best Swiss/German cooking in the Southland. Swiss style canneloni, Schnitzel a la Holstein, beef roulades and spaetzle are recommended. Outdoor garden dining.

Dinner: Tues.-Sun.	Reservations Recommended
Lunch: Tues.-Fri.	Cards: AE, DC, MC, V(BA)
Price: Moderate to Expensive	Valet Parking
Full Bar	

STUDIO GRILL   (213) 874-9202
7321 Santa Monica Blvd.
  (West of La Brea)
Hollywood

    The unusual is the usual at this off-beat store-front restaurant which hides behind a Pepsi Cola sign. Provocative dishes from all over the world, with a special nod to foods of the sea, are prepared with skill. Try the raspberry almond torte a la mode.

Dinner: Mon.-Sat.	Reservations Advised
Lunch: Mon.-Fri.	Cards: AE, DC, MC, V(BA)
Price: Moderate to Expensive	Street Parking
Wine and Beer	

TOP TEN RESTAURANTS FOR STEAK, CHICKEN, GUMBO AND OTHER AMERICAN FAVORITES IN LOS ANGELES/ORANGE COUNTIES

CLEARMAN'S GOLDEN COCK INN
7269 N. Rosemead   **(213) 287-1424**
(So. of Huntington Dr.)
San Gabriel

Big chicken dinners — broiled or fried — plus salad, cheese bread, huge baked potato, creamed spinach and onion rings. Still at bargain prices. Steaks are also a good value. Half portions of chicken for smaller appetites and children.

Dinner: Every Night   No Reservations
Price: Moderate   No Credit Cards
Full Bar   Parking Lot

COCK 'N BULL   **(213) 273-0081**
9170 Sunset Blvd.
(West of Doheny)
Sunset Strip, West Hollywood

Best all-you-can-eat buffet in the Southland features excellent prime rib, turkey, lamb curry, beef and kidney pie, etc. With it, Welsh Rarebit, salad, good desserts, coffee and English muffins and jam. Also outstanding Sunday brunch and famous bar (the Moscow Mule started here). A big-eaters delight.

Dinner: Every Night   Reservations Vital
Lunch: Mon.-Sat.   Major Cards
Brunch: Sun., 10-2:30   Valet Parking in Lot
Price: Moderate to Expensive
Full Bar

CORKSCREW RESTAURANT   **(213) 826-5501**
11647 San Vicente
(Near Barrington)
West Los Angeles

Corkscrew features two bars: one for generous drinks, the other an unusually good salad bar. A large, attractive restaurant with a reliable menu offering steaks, three cuts of prime rib, broiled chicken and Angler's Catch (fish of the day).

Dinner: Every Night   Reservations Recommended
Lunch: Mon.-Fri.   Cards: MC, V(BA)
Price: Moderate   Parking Garage
Full Bar

FIVE CROWNS   (714) 675-1374
3801 E. Coast Hwy.
Corona del Mar

The building and decor are English but the menu American in this attractive, well run restaurant which combines big drinks from a handsome bar, excellent food, friendly service and fair prices. Prime rib, roast duckling, rack of lamb, steaks, turbot, sherry chicken, strip sirloin and steak and crab are featured. On a warm night, ask to be seated in the garden patio.

Dinner: Mon.-Sat.	Reservations for Sure
Brunch: Sun., 10-2:30	Major Cards
Price: Moderate to Expensive	Parking Lot Across Street
Full Bar	

GALLEY STEAK HOUSE   (213) 399-9727
2442 Main Street
(So. of Pico)
Santa Monica

Marvelous steaks and clams in a funky nautical, ship-shape little place. We usually order one steak (they're huge) and a 3½-pound serving of Little Neck clams and stuff-up. Owner Ralph Stephan, who opened the Galley in 1934, is now in his eighties and still on the job. Crowded, but worth the wait.

Dinner: Every Night	No Reservations
Price: Moderate to Expensive	No Credit Cards
Full Bar	(Bring Cash) No Personal Checks
	Street Parking

HOMER AND EDY'S BISTRO   (213) 559-5102
2839 S. Robertson Blvd.
(No. of Santa Monica Fwy.)
Los Angeles

Native American cooking New Orleans style is served in this dressy little restaurant. Gumbo, oyster loaf, jambalaya and sweet potato pie are all featured.

Dinner: Tues.-Sun.	Reservations Advised
Price: Moderate to Expensive	Major Cards
Wine and Beer	Parking Lot in Rear

LAWRY'S THE PRIME RIB   (213) 652-2827
55 N. La Cienega Blvd.
(North of Wilshire)
Beverly Hills

Outstanding prime ribs carved at tableside from a gleaming 41 cart. Served with salad, Yorkshire pudding and creamed spinach. A family favorite.

Dinner: Every Night   No Reservations
Price: Moderate to Expensive   Major Cards
Full Bar   Valet Parking

NIEUPORT 17   (714) 547-9511
1615 East 17th Street
Santa Ana

Steak, prime rib, veal and shellfish served in a handsome restaurant filled with airplane memorabilia. Nice for lunch. Children's plates are an added attraction.

Dinner: Every Night   Reservations Recommended
Lunch: Mon.-Fri.   Major Cards
Price: Moderate to Expensive   Valet Parking
Full Bar

THE SALOON   (213) 273-7155
9390 Little Santa Monica
(East of Canon Drive)
Beverly Hills

Hidden behind the jammed action bar is a fine restaurant serving not only excellent basic American food but also unusual dishes with an international bent. Daily seafood specials are outstanding. Fine wine list at fair prices.

Dinner & Lunch: Mon.-Sat.   Reservations for Sure
Price: Moderate to Expensive   Major Cards
Full Bar   Street Parking

SYCAMORE INN   (714) 982-1104
Arroyo de los Osos (Bear Gulch)
8318 Foothill Blvd.
Cucamonga

This authentic circa-1900 California-style hacienda has become a Cucamonga institution. Grenadines of beef Theodora is the menu's star attraction. The food is consistently excellent. Remarkable wine list.

Dinner and Lunch: No Reservations accepted on
   Every Day   Saturdays; Recommended
Price: Moderate to Expensive   Other Days
Full Bar   Major Cards
                        Parking Lot

TOP TEN SEAFOOD RESTAURANTS OF
LOS ANGELES/ORANGE COUNTIES

CALABASAS INN   (213) 888-8870
23500 Park Sorrento Dr.
Calabasas Park

Local fish and seafood fresh from New England served in this spacious Spanish Colonial-style restaurant. Fun and different is the Clambake Dinner, Tuesday-Thursday. Outstanding selection of California wines.

Dinner: Tues.-Sun.	Reservations Recommended
Lunch: Tues.-Fri.	Major Cards
Brunch: Sun., 10-3	Valet Parking
Price: Moderate to Expensive	
Full Bar	

CRAB COOKER   (714) 673-0100
2200 Newport Blvd.
  (at 22nd)
Newport Beach

Granddaddy of the informal, charcoal brazier fish restaurants which now populate the area (Seafood Broiler, Walt's Wharf, etc.). Lotsa fresh fish. Also good clam chowder, sidewalk crab and shrimp cocktails. And lotsa fun.

Dinner & Lunch: Every Day	No Reservations
Lower Priced to Moderate	No Credit Cards
Beer and Wine	Street Parking

DELANEY'S SEA SHANTY   (714) 675-0100
630 Lido Park Drive
Newport Beach

Waterfront restaurant features quality fresh fish, simply but well prepared. Good anytime of the day. And the price is right. Busy.

Dinner & Lunch: Every Day	Reservations, 6 or More
Brunch: Sun., 9-3	Cards: MC, V(BA)
Price: Moderate	Public Lot Nearby
Full Bar	

Second Location:
841 El Toro Rd.   **(714) 830-6670**
Laguna Hills

MILLIE RIERRA'S SEAFOOD GROTTO
1700 Esplanade   (213) 375-1483
Redondo Beach
Seafood Italian-style is served in this handsome restaurant overlooking the Pacific. Dinners include relish tray, soup or salad and Pizza Siciliano. Good cocktails in casual bar with live background music.

Dinner & Lunch: Every Day	Reservations Recommended
Price: Moderate to Expensive	Major Cards
Full Bar	Small Parking Lot

NANTUCKET LIGHT   (213) 456-3105
22706 Pacific Coast Hwy.
Malibu
On a sandy beach centered on the curve of Santa Monica Bay, each table enjoys a great view. Lobster tails, Maine lobster, cioppino, Hangtown Fry and steamed clams. Steaks and prime rib for landlubbers.

Dinner: Every Night	No Reservations
Brunch: Sun., 10:30-2	Major Cards
Price: Moderate to Expensive	Parking Lot
Full Bar	

NOEL'S   (213) 592-2051
16281 Pacific Coast Hwy.
Seal Beach
Excellent fish dinners at bargain prices include potato, bread and salad or Manhattan chowder. One-pound Maine lobsters you can afford to enjoy. An outstanding deal. Unfortunately open only Friday through Sunday and closes early. Always jam-packed.

Dinners: Fri.-Sun.	No Reservations
Lower Priced	No Credit Cards
Full Bar/Entertainment	Parking Lot

PELICAN'S CATCH   (213) 392-5305
1715 Pacific Ave.
Venice
Fresh fish broiled or deep fried in non-cholesterol oil, plus low prices made Pelican's Catch a winner from the day it opened. Now, new Pelicans, following the same winning formula, are popping-up around the Southland.

Dinner: Every Night	No Reservations
Lunch: Tues.-Sun.	No Credit Cards
Lower Priced	Street Parking
Wine and Beer	

The Pelican   **(213) 545-6563**
3801 Highland Ave.   Lunch Reservations
Manhattan Beach   Cards: V(BA)

The Pelican's Roost   **(213) 988-6334**
8232 Sepulveda   No Reservations
  (near Roscoe)   Cards: V(BA)
Van Nuys

LE QUAI   **(213) 479-3779**
11835 Wilshire Blvd.
  (West of Barrington)
West Los Angeles
   You'll enjoy the Continental-style seafood dishes and understated decor. Favorite dishes are bouillabaisse, sand dabs Veronique and tarte toulonnaise — a delicious blend of seafood in cream sauce.

Dinner: Every Night	Reservations Vital
Price: Moderate to Expensive	Major Cards
Full Bar	Street Parking

SAND CASTLE   **(213) 457-9793**
22128 Pacific Coast Hwy.
  (in Pasadise Cove)
Malibu
   The sparkling Pacific Ocean and sandy beach of Paradise Cove makes a perfect setting for the Sand Castle — a hideaway restaurant which opens at 6 A.M. for fishermen's breakfasts and serves a varied menu all day. Seafood and fish are best.

Dinner, Lunch, Breakfast:	Reservations Advised
Every Day	Major Cards
Price: Moderate	Parking Lot
Full Bar	

THE SEASHELL   **(213) 884-6500**
19723 Ventura Blvd.
  (West of Corbin)
Tarzana
See "Top Ten Restaurants of Los Angeles/Orange Counties,"
   Page 30.

꧁꧂꧁꧂꧁꧂꧁꧂꧁꧂꧁꧂꧁꧂꧁꧂꧁꧂꧁꧂

TOP TEN ORIENTAL RESTAURANTS OF
LOS ANGELES/ORANGE COUNTIES

BANGKOK 1 RESTAURANT (Thai)
1253 N. La Brea Ave.   **(213) 876-9256**
Los Angeles

Los Angeles has its share of good Thai restaurants. They tend to be rather plain, but feature exciting food at good deal prices. Bangkok 1 is a good place to experiment with this complex cuisine. Ask for help in ordering — test different dishes and degrees of hotness.

Dinner & Lunch: Mon.-Sat.	Reservations Suggested
Lower Priced to Moderate	Cards: MC, V(BA)
Wine and Beer	Self Parking

FUJI GARDENS (Japanese)   (213) 393-2118
424 Wilshire Blvd.
(Between 4th and 5th)
Santa Monica

Beautifully prepared Japanese dinners include fresh sashimi or light and crispy tempura. Good service, pleasant atmosphere ...run with loving care. Special dinners can be ordered one day in advance.

Dinners: Tues.-Sun.	Reservations for Sure
Lunch: Tues.-Fri.	Cards: MC, V(BA)
Lower Priced to Moderate	Street Parking
Sake, Wine, Beer	

HUNAN (Northern Chinese)   (213) 626-5050
980 N. Broadway
Chinatown
Los Angeles

Plain restaurant with choice of 179 Chinese dishes on the menu. Many are unusual, and all are expertly prepared. Top recommendation.

Dinner and Lunch Daily	No Reservations
Lower Priced to Moderate	Cards: MC, V(BA)
No Liquor	Parking in Plaza Garage

KOTO (Japanese)   **(714) 752-7151**
4300 Van Karman Ave.
Newport Beach
   Beautiful Garden restaurant offers a variety of Japanese
dishes and rooms for each: Teppan dining in the Yaki Plum
Blossom Room, Sashimi in the Sushi Matsu Tie Pine Room,
and classic Japanese dishes in the formal dining room.

Dinner: Every Night   Reservations Advised
Lunch: Mon.-Fri.   Cards: MC, V(BA)
Price: Moderate to Expensive Parking Lot
Full Bar

MOULING GARDEN WEST (Northern Chinese)
11620 Wilshire Blvd.   **(213) 477-5041**
   (West of San Vicente)
West Los Angeles
   Excellent Szechwan and Mandarin dishes in a pleasant,
understated setting. Superior hot and sour soup, Mu Shu Pork,
Chinese chicken salad. Creative chef.

Dinner & Lunch: Every Day   Reservations Recommended
Lower Priced to Moderate   Major Cards
Full Bar   Validated Parking

Other Location:
Mouling   **(213) 464-4141**
6530 Sunset Blvd.
Hollywood

NEW PEKING (Korean)   **(213) 389-6764**
913½ So. Vermont
Wilshire District
Los Angeles
   The surprising thing about New Peking is that it is Korean
... the best Korean restaurant we know in the city. If you like
spicy-hot food — much of it from the sea — Korean cooking
could be your bag.

Dinner and Lunch: Fri.-Wed. Reservations Accepted
   (closed Thursday)   Cards: DC, MC, V(BA)
Lower Priced   Parking Lot
Beer, Sake

PANDA INN (Northern Chinese)
3472 E. Foothill Blvd.   **(213) 793-7300**
Pasadena
   The best Mandarin and Szechwan food in this part of the
city, and among the best anywhere in L.A. Try the three-flavor
and hot and sour soups, and spicy dishes. A good place to be   47

adventurous.

Dinner and Lunch Daily	Reservations Advised
Lower Priced to Moderate	Cards: MC, V(BA)
Full Bar, Rice Wine,	Parking Lot
Chinese Beer	

SHANGHAI WINTER GARDEN (Mandarin)
5651 Wilshire Blvd.   **(213) 934-0505**
(Between Fairfax and La Brea)
Miracle Mile, Los Angeles

Exceptional kitchen specializes in authentic Mandarin and provincial dishes. Spices handled with great expertise. Special dinners can be ordered in advance. Recently remodeled and enlarged.

Dinner and Lunch Daily	Reservations for Sure
Price: Moderate	Major Cards
Full Bar	Parking Lot

TOKYO KAIKAN (Japanese)   (213) 489-1333
225 So. San Pedro Street
Little Tokyo
Downtown Los Angeles

This favorite Japanese restaurant combines good food and good times. Everyone enjoys themselves as they eat or drink at one of the many bars (tempura, sushi, shabu-shabu, teppan or American cocktail). Or order from a varied menu in the main dining room.

Dinner: Mon.-Sat.	Reservations Recommended
Lunch: Mon.-Fri.	Major Cards
Price: Moderate	Parking Lot
Full Bar	

TWIN DRAGON (Northern Chinese)
8597 W. Pico Blvd.   **(213) 657-7355**
(West of La Cienega)
Los Angeles

Not much on decor here, but some delicious dishes. Try Twin Dragon's shrimp toast, hot and sour soup, and spicy chicken. All tops. 205 a la carte items plus complete dinners for 2 or more.

Dinner and Lunch Daily	Reservations, 6 or more
Lower Priced to Moderate	Major Cards
Full Bar	Parking Lot

Additional Twin Dragons:

1550 So. Harbor Blvd., Anaheim (714) 772-4400

20461 Ventura Blvd.	Brand New (no phone
Woodland Hills	at this writing)

TOP TEN INTERNATIONAL RESTAURANTS OF LOS ANGELES/ORANGE COUNTIES

AKBAR (Indian)   **(213) 822-4116**
590 Washington Street
Marina del Rey
    The cuisine of India served family-style — specializing in chicken, lamb, lobster and beef baked in a clay Tandoor oven. An ample selection of meat, seafood and vegetarian main dishes. Flavorful and different complete dinners with soup or salad, naar (Indian bread), daal (curried lentils), and raita (a yogurt spread).

Dinner & Lunch: Mon.-Sat.	Reservations Suggested
Price: Moderate	Cards: MC, V(BA)
Full Bar	Parking Lot

CANO'S (Mexican Seafood)   **(714) 631-1381**
2241 W. Coast Hwy.
Newport Beach
    "Seafoods of Mexico" are the specialty in this new waterfront showplace. Try the snapper Veracruz stuffed with shrimp and crab. Or unique lobster, crab, shrimp and pompano dishes. Also ceviche, angualas and tortilla soup. Spectacular bar.

Dinner: Every Night	Reservations for
Lunch: Mon.-Sat.	Sunday Lunch Only
Special Sunday Lunch: 10-3	Cards: AE, MC, V(BA)
Price: Expensive	Valet Parking
Full Bar	

EL CHAVO (Mexican)   **(213) 664-0871**
4441 Sunset Blvd.
    (East of Virgil/Hillhurst)
Hollywood
    Perfect combination of zesty Mexican food, interesting menu, easy service. Lively and light-hearted feeling. Generous portions at value prices. Piano and/or guitar music most nights.

Dinner and Lunch Daily	Reservations Advised
Lower Priced to Moderate	No Credit Cards
Full Bar/Piano or Guitar	Parking Lot

THE COVE (German plus Continental dishes)
3191 W. 7th St.   (213) 388-0361
(Just East of Ambassador Hotel)
Wilshire District, Los Angeles

Dressy, reasonably priced and quietly romantic restaurant with roaming violinist and piano in the bar. Serves a varied menu, but German food is the specialty. Rahmschnitzel, sauerbraten and weiner schnitzel with German fried potatoes are recommended.

Dinner: Every Night	Reservations Recommended
Lunch: Mon.-Fri.	Major Cards
Price: Moderate to Expensive	Valet Parking
Full Bar	

KAVKAZ (Russian)   (213) 652-6582
8795 Sunset Blvd.
(across from Tower Records)
Sunset Strip, West Hollywood

Enjoy a sparkling view of L.A. while savoring rack of lamb marinated in pomegranate juice (Sedlo). The menu is not large, but all dishes are authentic and well prepared. The Markarian family combine their talents to make Kavkaz "tops" for Russian.

Dinner: Tues.-Sun.	Reservations Advised
Price: Moderate	Major Cards
Full Bar	Parking Lot

LA MASIA (Spanish)   (213) 273-7066
9077 Santa Monica Blvd.
(East of Doheny)
West Hollywood

Soft lights, greenery and intimate rooms create a romantic setting for L.A.'s top Spanish restaurant. Paella, stuffed breast of chicken, unusual seafood and vegetarian dishes are featured.

Dinner: Every Night	Reservations Advised
Price: Moderate	Cards: AE, MC, V(BA)
Full Bar	Street Parking

PAPADAKIS TAVERNA (Greek)
301 W. 6th Street   (213) 548-1186
(East of Gaffey)
San Pedro

See "Top Ten Restaurants of Los Angeles/Orange Counties,"
Page 29

THE PARAGON (Yugoslavian) (213) 831-2200
660 W. 7th Street
  (East of Gaffey)
San Pedro

This small, family run restaurant is a top choice for several reasons: the excellent homemade soups, bread and rolls, a dish called "Jijeskavica" (chopped beef, onions, spices...and delicious), and supreme apple strudel. The Milojevcic's run the Paragon with care, Zarko looks after customers, while Tanya rules the kitchen.

Dinner: Tues.-Sun.	Reservations Accepted
Lower Priced to Moderate	Street Parking
Wine and Beer	

THE SHAH (Afghanistan) (213) 379-4849
124 N. Sepulveda Blvd.
Manhattan Beach

The Shah's menu tells us some of the dishes go back thousands of years and have been enjoyed by the likes of Cyrus the Great and Genghis Khan. You can enjoy them today — comfortably seated on cushions in a living room atmosphere. Fine kabobs, best dolma (ground meat in grape leaves) we've tasted. All vegetables are fresh. Children's dinners.

Dinner: Wed.-Sun.	Reservations Accepted
Price: Moderate	Cards: MC, V(BA)
Wine and Beer	Parking Lot

STRATTON'S (English) (213) 477-4907
10886 Le Conte Ave.
  (East of Westwood Blvd.)
Westwood Village

This classy little restaurant occupies a portion of the handsome, one-time Masonic Lodge in Westwood and demonstrates English cooking can be outstanding. Stratton's Quiche Lorraine is the best we know of in L.A. Also trout, prime rib, lamb chops, duckling. Pleasant outdoor patio.

Dinner and Lunch: Tues.-Sun.	Reservations Advised
Price: Moderate to Expensive	Cards: MC, V(BA)
Full Bar	Self Parking

APPLE PAN   (213) 474-9344
11801 W. Pico Blvd.
   (East of Westwood Blvd.)
West Los Angeles

   Lots of good hamburgers in L.A., but our favorite is the miniscule, counter-only Apple Pan. Also, good ham sandwiches and fruit pies. Slogan is, "Quality Forever," and they mean it.

Open Daily	No Reservations
Lower Priced	No Cards
No Liquor	Small Parking Lot

DELANEY'S KETTLE OF FISH (714) 675-3145
632 Lido Park Place
Newport Beach

   Sit in the sun, watch the harbor action, and enjoy good fresh fish and chowder from this seafood snack kitchen next to the larger Delaney's Sea Shanty. Great on a sunny afternoon.

Open Daily	No Reservations
Lower Priced	No Cards
Wine and Beer	Parking Lot

Other Locations:
280 So. Coast Hwy.   **(714) 494-6353**
Laguna Beach

23696 El Toro Rd.   **(714) 581-3511**
El Toro

DELI DEPOT   (213) 344-7131
18395 Ventura Blvd.
   (East of Reseda)
Tarzana

   Hidden behind Bob's is a new and terrific Kosher-style deli. Big, big sandwiches and platters, well made with quality ingredients. Best deli buy in L.A.

Dinner, Lunch, Breakfast:	No Reservations
Every Day	Cards: MC, V(BA)
Lower Priced	Parking Lot
Wine and Beer	

52

JOE ALLEN'S   (213) 274-7144
8706 W. 3rd Street
  (East of Robertson)
Los Angeles
   Same menu served daily from 11:30 a.m. to 1:00 a.m.
Blackboard menu includes chili, BBQ chicken and ribs, salads,
steaks, liver and onions. Informal but hectic place. Where the
action is.

Dinner, Lunch, Supper Daily   Reservations Recommended
Lower Priced to Moderate   Cards: MC, V(BA)
Full Bar   Valet Parking

JOSEPHINA'S   (213) 553-6955
10369 Santa Monica Blvd.
  (East of Beverly Glen)
Century City Area
   Deep dish pizza and 1920's setting are featured in this West
L.A. showplace. Food is good, decor and atmosphere lively.
Good place for children . . . and after-theatre supper. Entertain-
ers are young and talented.

Dinner: Every Night   No Reservations
Lunch: Mon.-Sat.   Major Cards
Lower Priced to Moderate   Valet Parking
Full Bar

Additional Location:
13562 Ventura Blvd.   (213) 990-0411
Sherman Oaks

MARIE CALLENDER'S
Many Locations throughout
  Los Angeles and Orange Counties
   This formula chain-restaurant does a much needed job with
hamburgers, chili melt, soups, corn bread and pies. Newer
$1,000,000-plus units are loaded with ornamental decorations,
and have a full bar service.

Dinner and Lunch Daily   No Reservations
Lower Priced to Moderate   Cards: MC, V(BA)
Full Bar in Newer Units   Parking Lots

Other Locations in San Diego, Sacramento, and Santa Clara
    Counties . . . and still growing.

RAZZLE DAZZLE   (213) 829-5303
2226 Wilshire Blvd.
   (Between 22nd and 23rd)
Santa Monica

Innovative sandwiches and creative salads plus bean sprouts and fresh fruit are the trademark of Razzle Dazzle. Try the turkey and avocado tostada, or "The devil made me do it" salad (turkey, bacon, avocado, mushrooms, cottage cheese, etc. etc.).

Dinner: Every Night   Reservations (Dinner Only)
Lunch: Mon.-Fri.   Cards: AE, MC, V(BA)
Brunch: Sat., Sun. 11-3   Parking Lot
Lower Priced to Moderate
Wine and Beer

SEA 'N SHORE   (213) 399-5552
205 Ocean Front Walk
   (Between Rose and Navy)
Venice

This French bistro by the bay sits on the beach and serves some of L.A.'s best omelettes and crepe dishes. Outdoor tables for sunny days and balmy nights. Continental dinners...fresh apple or banana beignets.

Dinner and Lunch Daily   Reservations Advised
Breakfast: Summer Only   Cards: AE, V(BA)
Lower Priced to Moderate   Street Parking
Wine and Beer

STERN'S BARBECUE   (213) 871-0950
12658 Washington Blvd.
Culver City

    Consistently good BBQ. Meaty sandwiches, chicken and ribs with a zesty sauce. Congenial Western-style informality. Quality and quantity make this tops.

Dinner and Lunch Daily	No Reservations
Lower Priced to Moderate	Cards: MC, V(BA)
Full Bar/Guitarist Fri., Sat.	Parking Lot

YELLOWFINGERS   (213) 990-1791
15013 Ventura Blvd.
(East of Sepulveda)
Sherman Oaks

    Yellowfingers is the Valley's bistro. It has real charm. Plus crepes, superlative salads, thick onion soup, escargot, ratatouille . . . fancy desserts and espresso, served all day.

Dinner and Lunch: Mon.-Sat.	Reservations for Sure
Lower Priced to Moderate	Cards: MC, V(BA)
Full Bar	Street Parking

Other Location:

22616 Ventura Blvd.   **(213) 990-1791**
(West of Topanga Canyon)
Woodland Hills

TOP TEN GOOD DEAL RESTAURANTS OF
LOS ANGELES/ORANGE COUNTIES

ANDRE'S OF BEVERLY HILLS (213) 657-2446
8635 Wilshire Blvd.
Beverly Hills

Complete Continental dinners are expertly prepared, professionally served and are huge — antipasto, soup, salad, pasta, entree and dessert. Always crowded.

Dinner: Tues.-Sun.	Reservations Advised
Lunch: Tues.-Fri.	Major Cards
Price: Moderate	Valet Parking
Full Bar	

BARRAGAN'S   (213) 628-4520
1538 W. Sunset Blvd.
(East of Alvarado)
Los Angeles

Big breakfast-lunch-dinner-supper. A very Mexican restaurant serves everything from tacos to shrimp and eggs. We like the machaca burritos, Ropa Vieja, Carne Adobada. Ask the cheerful waitresses to translate.

Dinner, Breakfast, Lunch	Reservations Accepted
Daily	Cards: MC, V(BA)
Lower Priced	Street Parking
Full Bar/Music	

CARL ANDERSEN'S CHATAM   (213) 479-1776
10930 Weyburn Avenue
Westwood Village

Extensive varied menu in the Danish manner. Many daily specials. Andersen cooks and writes menus with integrity. Promotes his chicken salad as "made with turkey since 1939."

Dinner and Lunch: Mon.-Sat.	Reservations for Dinner
Lower Priced to Moderate	Cards: MC, V(BA)
Full Bar	Street Parking

THE GYPSY   (213) 451-2841
1215 4th Street
(So. of Wilshire)
Santa Monica

This tiny restaurant serves Anglo-Indian style curry dishes. If you show interest, the enthusiastic owners Tina and Tom

Todd will explain the preparation, ingredients and origin of each.

Dinner: Tues.-Sun.	Reservations Advised
Lower Priced to Moderate	Cards: MC, V(BA)
No Liquor	Street Parking

HEART OF EUROPE (213) 467-8910
476 N. Western Avenue
** (No. of Beverly)**
Wilshire District
Los Angeles

Roast duck, chicken paprika, beef goulash on complete dinners including hors d'oeuvre, soup, salad, and dessert — all in a festive mood. Karel Finek hosts while doubling on piano and organ. Jarina runs the bountiful kitchen.

Dinner: Wed.-Mon.	Reservations Recommended
Lower Priced	No Credit Cards
Wine, Beer and Music	Parking Lot

LA PARISIENNE (213) 443-5535
2905 N. Durfee Avenue
El Monte

Owners of this off-the-beaten-path restaurant have successfully created a French inn. Seafood and veal are the specialties and Friday bouillabaisse is outstanding.

Dinner: Tues.-Sun.	Reservations Accepted
Price: Moderate	Major Cards
Wine	Parking Lot

LE PETITE SWISS (213) 478-9223
1383 Westwood Blvd.
** (So. of Wilshire)**
West Los Angeles

Italian and German-style veal dishes, plus French-style seafood represent the three sections of Switzerland. Dinners include relish tray, good soup or salad. Tiny and popular.

Dinner: Mon.-Sat.	Reservations Advised
Lower Priced to Moderate	Cards: AE, MC, V(BA)
Wine and Beer	Street Parking

LA STREGA   (213) 385-1546
400 So. Western
Wilshire District
Los Angeles

A swell selection of pasta with zesty sauces and super pizza in an attractive old world setting. All this, plus piano music and reasonable prices, make La Strega a "best buy."

Dinner: Every Night	Reservations Recommended
Lunch: Mon.-Sat.	Cards: MC, V(BA)
Lower Priced to Moderate	Parking Lot
Wine and Beer	

VICKMAN'S   (213) 622-3852
1228 E. 8th Street
Downtown Los Angeles

Where can you eat at 3 a.m.? Vickman's, which is next door to the Produce Market. Two big, plain rooms with long tables. Not much. But quality of food is tops, portions ample and prices a bargain. Famous fresh strawberry pie (in season).

Open Mon.-Fri.,	No Reservations
3 a.m.-3 p.m.	No Credit Cards
Lower Priced	Parking Lot
Beer	

WALT'S WHARF   (213) 598-4433
201 Main Street
Seal Beach

"If it's fresher, it's still swimming," is Walt's claim for his seafood. The fish is excellent and flavorfully charcoal broiled. The kind we like.

Dinner and Lunch Daily	No Reservations
Lower Priced	Cards: MC, V(BA)
Wine and Beer	Parking Lot

TOP TEN SPECIAL INTEREST RESTAURANTS OF LOS ANGELES/ORANGE COUNTIES

EL GATO   **(213) 781-1580**
7424 N. Sepulveda
  (No. of Sherman Way)
Van Nuys
   This combination Mexican restaurant/night club pairs good Tex-Mex food at reasonable prices with Mexican entertainment. Good family fun. Call for show schedules and details.

Dinner and Lunch Daily   Reservations Suggested
Lower Priced to Moderate   Cards: AE, MC, V(BA)
Full Bar   Parking Lot

FARMER'S MARKET   **(213) 933-9211**
3rd St. and Fairfax   **(for information)**
Los Angeles
   So much fun, locals don't let tourists scare them away. Unique shopping with outdoor dining. Great variety of foods and baked goods. Also fine produce, seafood, meats, sweets and cheeses.

Open Mon.-Sat.   Credit Cards: Varies by
June-Oct.: 9 a.m.-8 p.m.   Vendor. Mostly cash.
Nov.-May: 9 a.m.-6:30 p.m.   Parking Lot
Closed holidays

GRISWOLD'S COMPLEX   **(714) 626-2411**
555 W. Foothill Blvd.
  (and vicinity)
Claremont
   Interesting complex includes a pleasant and handsome Spanish Colonial style restaurant (Griswold's Indian Hill), smorgasbord, Mexican restaurant, bakery, gift shop, motel and the old Claremont High School converted into shops and eateries.

Open: Every Day   Call for Details
   Lunch and Dinner   Parking Lot

KNOTT'S BERRY FARM   (714) 827-1776
8039 Beach Blvd.
   (2 mi. so. of Santa Ana Frwy.)
Buena Park
   Knott's started as a berry stand, turned into a restaurant, then evolved into a shopping center/amusement park. But their chicken dinners remain a star attraction for both quality and value. There's also a steak restaurant, but it's Knott's Chicken House that's the best deal.

Dinner and Lunch Daily	No Reservations
Lower Priced	No Credit Cards
No Liquor	Parking Lot

LAWRY'S CALIFORNIA CENTER
Ave. 26 at San Fernando Rd.   (213) 225-2491
   (phone for directions)
Downtown Los Angeles
   Outdoor dining in a magnificent Spanish Colonial garden paradise is a memorable Southern California experience. Only barbecued Delmonico steaks are served, along with salad and vegetables. Beautiful cocktail terrace. Wine shop sells California's best at regular retail prices. Add $1.50 corkage and enjoy it with dinner. Unusual lunches are also served.

Dinner: Wed.-Sun.,	Reservations: 6 or more
May through October	Cards: AE, MC, V(BA)
Lunch: Mon.-Sat.	Parking Lot
Price: Moderate to Expensive	
Full Bar	

THE RANCH HOUSE   (805) 646-2360
102 Besant Rd.
Ojai
   Garden and indoor dining features original recipes using fresh fruits and vegetables and herbs with chicken, pork, beef, seafood, etc. Fine soups, salads and desserts. Beautiful area.

Dinner: Wed.-Sun.	Reservations Vital
Price: Moderate to Expensive	No Cards
Wine and Beer	Parking Lot

REDONDO BEACH PIER   (213) 374-3481
Harbor Drive   **(for information)**
Redondo Beach

L.A.'s version of Fisherman's Wharf is the Redondo Beach waterfront which includes King Harbor, Portofino Marina and the Redondo Municipal Pier. View restaurants plus good browsing, shopping and snacking on the Pier. A swell place on a warm afternoon or evening.

THE TOWER   (213) 746-1554
Occidental Center
1150 S. Olive St.
  (between 11th and 12th)
Downtown Los Angeles

One of L.A.'s best French restaurants is also L.A.'s best view restaurant. The sunset view can be spectacular. Ditto for the seafood.

Dinner: Mon.-Sat.	Reservations Advised
Lunch: Mon.-Fri.	Major Cards
Price: Expensive to Very	Valet Parking
Full Bar	Dress: Jackets

VICTORIA STATION   (213) 760-0754
(100 Universal City Plaza)
3850 Lankershim Blvd.
Universal City

This $3,500,000+ Victoria Station is the prime rib chain's showplace ... and it's something to see. The simulated station includes the famous four-sided clock first installed in the original Victoria Station in 1860, plus four cars from the Flying Scotsman. Good prime rib and salad bar plus some excellent California wine values.

Dinner and Lunch Daily	Reservations: 6 or more
Price: Moderate	Major Cards
Full Bar	Parking Lot

THE WAREHOUSE   **(213) 823-5451**
4499 Admiralty Way
Marina del Rey

   The Warehouse epitomizes the Marina del Rey restaurant
— limited menu of American favorites with fancied-up names,
active bars and magnificient views of the Marina's boating
action. The Warehouse takes more care with food than most,
and adds the atmosphere of a South Seas harbor-side warehouse.

Dinner: Every Night	Reservations: 8 or more
Lunch: Mon.-Fri.	Major Cards
Brunch: Sun., 10:30-2:30	Parking Lot
Price: Moderate	
Full Bar	

Other Locations:
The Warehouse   **(714) 673-4700**
3450 Via Oporto
Lido Village, Newport Beach

Beachbum Burt's   **(213) 376-0466**
605 N. Harbor Drive
Redondo Beach

TOP TEN SALOONS AND
OTHER GREAT PLACES FOR A DRINK IN
LOS ANGELES/ORANGE COUNTIES

BEL AIR HOTEL　　　　　　**(213) 472-1211**
701 Stone Canyon Rd.
Bel Air, Los Angeles
　　Romantic garden setting in a mansion-studded neighbor-hood evokes the Southern California dream. Entertainment Tuesday through Sunday evening.

BERGIN'S WEST　　　　　　**(213) 820-3641**
11600 San Vicente Blvd.
Brentwood, Los Angeles
　　Currently, L.A.'s most congested and active bar — more bodies than Coney Island on an August Sunday afternoon. Also famous for Irish Coffee.

THE TOP OF FIVE　　　　　　**(213) 624-1000**
Bonaventure Hotel
333 So. Flower
Downtown Los Angeles
　　This circular, revolving cocktail lounge turns slowly on the 35th Floor of L.A.'s spectacular new hotel, revealing a 360° panoramic view of Los Angeles. Best at sunset.

GORDA LIZ　　　　　　**(714) 675-5111**
900 Bayside Dr.
Newport Beach
　　The downstairs bar in this Portuguese-style fisherman's house is a marvelous setting for a very good martini — which happens to be the beautifully presented house specialty.

HOLIDAY HOUSE　　　　　　**(213) 457-3641**
27400 Pacific Coast Hwy.
　(So. of Paradise Cove)
Malibu
　　Oceanfront patio terraces towards the Pacific below. Spec-tacular view from this romantic hideaway.

LAWRY'S CALIFORNIA CENTER
Ave. 26 at San Fernando Rd.   **(213) 225-2491**
Downtown Los Angeles

Sip cocktails in a beautiful Spanish Colonial garden setting complete with fountains and Mariachis. The Los Angeles experience. Open Wednesday through Sunday from 3 p.m.

POLO LOUNGE   **(213) 276-2251**
Beverly Hills Hotel
9641 W. Sunset
Beverly Hills

From lunch through the cocktail hour, this is where Hollywood goes to see and be seen. Frantic, noisy atmosphere right out of the movies.

QUIET CANNON   **(714) 496-6146**
34344 Street of the Green Lantern
  (just off the Coast Hwy.)
Dana Point

The cocktail terrace of this cliff-side restaurant has both a dramatic view of the Dana Point Marina and an authentic salvaged Spanish cannon.

EL TORITO   **(213) 823-8941**
13737 Fiji Way
  (at Fisherman's Village)
Marina del Rey

Situated directly on the main channel, El Torito's cocktail lounge provides the best look at the Marina's boating action. Top label well drinks. Hors d'oeuvres 3-6, Monday through Saturday.

VICTOR HUGO INN   **(714) 494-9477**
361 Cliff Drive
Laguna Beach

The cocktail terrace of Victor Hugo's sits amid one of the world's beautiful settings: Laguna Beach's flower-filled, ocean-front park in the foreground; the clean, white beaches and blue, blue Pacific, the backdrop. A personal favorite.

TOP TEN RESTAURANTS OF
THE SAN FRANCISCO BAY AREA

DORO'S   (415) 397-6822
714 Montgomery Street
   (near Washington)
Financial District, San Francisco
   Doro's is a big, busy, sophisticated San Francisco restaurant
whose hallmark is "consistency." Its drinks are honest, food
carefully prepared from quality ingredients, portions generous,
service professional, atmosphere festive. Doro's is enjoyable for
dinner, but a San Francisco institution at lunch. Mostly Northern Italian and Continental dishes. Marvelous pasta, chicken
and veal. Fresh fish prepared at its best. The skillful chef also
creates daily specials. Wonderful wine list.

Dinner: Mon.-Sat.   Reservations for Sure
Lunch: Mon.-Fri.   Major Cards
Price: Expensive   Valet Parking
Full Bar

FOURNOU'S OVENS   (415) 989-1910
Stanford Court Hotel
905 California
   (at Powell) Nob Hill, San Francisco
   One of San Francisco's most handsome and subtly elegant
restaurants...tiled and terraced to create a unique setting.
From the "ovens" come rack of lamb, sauce aux aromates;
roast duckling with green peppercorns and kumquat sauce and
roast capon a L'Estragon. Plus a selection of superlative seafood and meat dishes. Vegetables are expertly prepared.
Fournou's Ovens is one of a few remaining outstanding hotel
restaurants. Exceptional list of California wines.

Dinner: Every Night   Reservations Advised
Price: Expensive   Major Cards
Excellent Full Bar   Valet Parking
                             Dress: Jackets

MAMA'S
Washington Square   **(415) 362-6421**
Union Square (Macy's)   **(415) 391-3790**
Nob Hill (Grovesnor Towers) **(415) 928-1004**
San Mateo (Macy's)   **(415) 573-1176**
See "Top Ten Restaurants of California," Pages 26-27.

65

LA MIRABELLE   (415) 421-3374
1326 Powell
  (So. of Broadway)
North Beach, San Francisco

The kitchen is the star attraction of this stylish San Francisco French restaurant. Classic veal dishes, scampi, fresh seafood and lamb are all outstanding. For openers, try their light quenelles, the escargot or the Barquette des Fruits de Mer... and for dessert, a superb souffle or tarte tatin. At Mirabelle an evening of gaiety and gourmet foods are enhanced by the concerned staff.

Dinner: Tues.-Sat.	Reservations Vital
Price: Expensive	Major Cards
Full Bar	Valet Parking
	Dress: Jackets

NARSAI'S   (415) 527-7900
385 Colusa
  (North of Berkeley)
Kensington

Narsai David has created a unique California restaurant using the redwood stays and iron fittings from a huge water tank which once stood high in the Oakland Hills. The result is not rustic, but a modern sophisticated setting for the full course dinners he prepares with care and serves with elegance. Rack of lamb Assyrien (marinated in Pomegranate), veal sweetbreads, medallions of veal, and the fresh fish dishes (especially salmon in season) are excellent choices. Dinners include appetizer, outstanding soup, entree, then salad and dessert and coffee. Special dinners are featured Monday nights. Extensive wine list.

Dinner: Every Night	Reservations Advised
Price: Expensive to Very	Major Cards
Full Bar	Parking Lot

L'ORANGERIE   (415) 776-3600
419 O'Farrell
  (between Taylor and Jones)
Downtown San Francisco
See "Top Ten Restaurants of California," Pages 8-9.

RISTORANTE ORSI   **(415) 981-6535**
375 Bush Street
   (Between Kearny & Montgomery)
Financial District, San Francisco
See "Top Ten Restaurants of California," Pages 12-13.

TADICH GRILL   **(415) 391-2373**
240 California Street   **No Reservations**
   (near Front)
Financial District, San Francisco
See "Top Ten Restaurants of California," Pages 20-21.

TRADER VIC'S   **(415) 653-3400**
9 Anchor Drive
Watergate Complex
Emeryville

   The Emeryville Trader Vic's is the direct descendent of the
Oakland original, and the Trader we like best. All three California Trader Vic's are first class, but Emeryville has an easy
style which makes you feel more relaxed than its San Francisco
and Beverly Hills counterparts. It's also less expensive. And
beautifully appointed in its waterfront setting. The menu is far
more than Polynesian. It has a genuine International menu —
Cantonese, Malaysian, Indian, French and Continental dishes.
All skillfully prepared. "Trader Vic" Bergeron, of course, is
also creator of the Mai Tai and Fog Cutter and one of the great
restaurateurs of America.

Dinner: Every Night   Reservations Vital
Lunch: Mon.-Fri.   Major Cards
Price: Moderate to Expensive   Parking Lot
Full Bar, Excellent Wine List

Other Location:
10 Cosmo Place   **(415) 776-2232**
   (off Taylor near Post)
Downtown San Francisco

                    Dress: Jacket and Tie

YET WAH   (415) 387-8040
1801, 1829 and 2140 Clement St.
Richmond District, San Francisco

Yet Wah's instant success has already sprouted into five locations — three of them on a short stretch of Clement Street. Why this popularity? First, a 301-item menu...mostly beautifully prepared Northern Chinese dishes (a logistical triumph in the kitchen). Second, reasonable prices. Third, pleasant atmosphere and service. Try Yet Wah's superb Princess Garden Chicken Salad or the fried half duck with steamed buns and plum sauce.

Dinner: Every Night	Reservations Recommended
Lower Priced to Moderate	Major Cards
Bar Service: Varies by	Street Parking
Location	

Other Locations:

5238 Diamond Heights Blvd.   (415) 282-0404
San Francisco

505 Strawberry Town and   (415) 388-2412
Country Village
Mill Valley

TOP TEN FRENCH RESTAURANTS OF
THE SAN FRANCISCO BAY AREA

COW HOLLOW INN   (415) 922-2777
2221 Filbert Street
  (Between Steiner and Fillmore)
Cow Hollow, San Francisco

The Cow Hollow Inn is French, gracious and affordable. It's a small, chic two-story restaurant where talented chef Paul Dufour prepares some of San Francisco's best French dishes. Seafood, sweetbreads, rack of lamb and filet mignon with mustard sauce. No cocktails, but good wine and aperitif list.

Dinner: Mon.-Sat.	Reservations Advised
Lunch: Mon.-Fri.	Cards: MC, V(BA)
Price: Moderate to Expensive	Valet Parking
Wine and Beer	Dress: Jackets

LA CROISETTE   (415) 981-1176
745 Columbus Avenue
  (near Fillbert)
North Beach, San Francisco

New and already among San Francisco's top French restaurants, La Croisette is the North Beach creation of Maurice Estarellas. Several unusual, excellent dishes (trout in port, duckling, boned and marinated in wine and herbs), an outstanding bouillabaisse. Very attractive.

Dinner: Mon.-Sat.	Reservations Recommended
Price: Expensive	Cards: MC, V(BA)
Wine and Beer	Self Parking

LE CYRANO   (415) 387-1090
4134 Geary Blvd.
  (between 6th and 7th Ave.)
Richmond District, San Francisco

Charming Madame Bovigny runs this very French restaurant which is so popular that weekend reservations should be made well ahead. Veal, beef, rack of lamb, duckling, and seafood are featured. Portions are large and prices reasonable.

Complete dinners include soup, salad, dessert and coffee.
Everyone likes Le Cyrano.

Dinner: Mon.-Sat.	Reservations Vital
(closed month of July)	No Credit Cards
Price: Moderate	Street Parking
Full Bar	

CHEZ JON   (415) 922-1211
3673 Sacramento Street
   (Between Spruce and Locust)
Presidio Heights, San Francisco
   Chez Jon is an American's expression of what a San Francisco French restaurant should be. And the result is most suc-
cessful. Jon Sihler has created an intimate country inn, and
serves excellent French fare. It's a place that makes you feel
good. Enjoy the garden on sunny days.

Dinner: Tues.-Sun.	Reservations Advised
Lunch: Tues.-Fri.	Cards: MC, V(BA)
Price: Moderate	Street Parking
Wine and Beer	

CHEZ JOSEPH   (415) 444-6183
567 Fifth Street
   (on Bret Harte Boardwalk)
Oakland
   Located in a restored Victorian building that's well past its
100th birthday, Chez Joseph is one of the best restaurants in
East Bay. The menu is short but features a range from seafood
to veal, chicken to beef. Good wine list.

Dinner: Tues.-Sat.	Reservations Advised
Lunch: Tues.-Fri.	Cards: D, MC, V(BA)
Price: Moderate to Expensive	Street Parking
Wine and Beer	

FLEUR DE LYS   (415) 673-7779
777 Sutter
   (between Jones and Taylor)
Downtown, San Francisco
   Fleur de Lys is one San Francisco restaurant that goes all
out for dramatic good looks as well as fine food. The canopied
ceiling suggests the tent of an Arab sheik, (with oil wells). The

veal here is especially recommended. Dinners are a la carte —
food and service are excellent.

Dinner: Tues.-Sun.   Reservations for Sure
Price: Expensive to Very   Major Cards
Full Bar   Valet Parking
                                  Dress: Jackets

LA MIRABELLE   (415) 421-3374
1326 Powell
  (So. of Broadway)
North Beach, San Francisco
See "Top Ten Restaurants of San Francisco," Page 66.

L'ORANGERIE   (415) 776-3600
419 O'Farrell
  (between Taylor and Jones)
Downtown San Francisco
See "Top Ten Restaurants of California," Pages 8-9.

LA POTINIERE   (415) 664-0655
2305 Irving Street
  (at 24th Avenue)
Sunset District, San Francisco
   This attractive country-style restaurant features well exe-
cuted dishes at most reasonable prices. Canard aux peches and
sweetbreads in port and cream are star attractions. Also, homemade Napoleons. Distinctive — a top recommendation.

Dinner: Tues.-Sat.   Reservations Advised
Price: Moderate   Cards: MC, V(BA)
Wine and Beer   Street Parking

LA TERRASSE   (415) 494-0700
3740 El Camino Real
Palo Alto
   The menu of this country French restaurant is accented by
some Belgian dishes like fondue de fromage Bruxelloise, a
superb appetizer. Excellent seafood plus veal, rack of lamb,
duckling and beef dishes. Attractive atmosphere. Patio dining
when weather permits.

Dinner: Mon.-Sat.   Reservations Recommended
Lunch: Mon.-Fri.   Cards: MC, V(BA)
Price: Moderate to Expensive   Self Parking
Full Bar

TOP TEN ITALIAN RESTAURANTS OF
THE SAN FRANCISCO BAY AREA

DORO'S   **(415) 397-6822**
714 Montgomery Street
    (near Washington)
Financial District, San Francisco
See "Top Ten Restaurants of San Francisco," Page 65.

EDUARDO'S   **(415) 567-6164**
2234 Chestnut
    (near Pierce)
Marina District, San Francisco
    Great, made-fresh-daily pasta. Fabulous fettucine and tortellini. Zesty and unusual sauces. Also superior Saltimbocca. This tiny, no reservation restaurant is always jammed.

Dinner: Tues.-Sat.	No Reservations
(closed from mid-May to	No Credit Cards
July 5th)	Street Parking
Price: Moderate	
Wine and Beer	

GUIDO'S   **(415) 982-2157**
347 Columbus Avenue
    (above Broadway)
North Beach, San Francisco
    San Francisco is famous for good Italian food, still Guido's stands out. It's a small, personal place which exudes Italian charm. It reflects the personality of owner Guido Piccinina, a first class restaurateur. We like veal a la Guido, prawns Dijonnaise and chicken Toscana. Lots of nice extras.

Dinner: Tues.-Sat.	Reservations Essential
Price: Moderate to Expensive	Cards: MC, V(BA)
Wine, Aperitifs	Street Parking

LORENZO'S RISTORANTE ITALIANO
729 Sir Francis Drake Blvd.   (415) 453-2552
San Anselmo
   Fresh clams and mussels flown from the east, white veal, and excellent sauces make Lorenzo's Marin's finest Italian restaurant. Pleasant atmosphere, good service.

Dinner: Tues.-Sun.	Reservations Advised
Lunch: Tues.-Sat.	Cards: AE, MC, V(BA)
Brunch: Sun., 10-2	Valet Parking
Price: Moderate	
Wine and Beer	

NORTH BEACH RESTAURANT
1512 Stockton   (415) 392-1700
** (at Columbus)**
North Beach, San Francisco
   North Beach epitomizes the "San Francisco-style Italian Restaurant" — always crowded, big dinners and reasonable. Complete dinners from antipasto to dessert and beverage. A giant menu. Favorite dish is Veal alla Bruno con Pinoli, (pine nuts and mushrooms).

Dinner and Lunch Daily	Reservations Vital
Price: Moderate to Expensive	Major Cards
Full Bar	Valet Parking

RISTORANTE ORSI   (415) 981-6535
375 Bush Street
** (Between Kearny and Montgomery)**
Financial District, San Francisco
See "Top Ten Restaurants of California," Pages 12-13.

PAPA D. CARLO'S   (415) 376-2533
337 Rheem Blvd.
Moraga
   Papa D. Carlo's is a Northern California transplant from Los Angeles which serves a set-menu dinner — good and BIG: nine courses . . . maybe more, depending on how you count. With an intermission for stretching at the halfway point. Go and enjoy your "Papa Dinner."

Dinner: Tues.-Sun.	Reservations Essential
(seating between 6PM	Cards: MC, V(BA)
& 9PM)	Parking Lot
Price: Moderate	
Wine	

IL PAVONE   (415) 548-0400
1730 Shattuck Avenue
Berkeley

    An intimate dining room — brick walls painted white, dark beams, understated. Cuisine of Northern Italy is skillfully cooked and served. Calamari, melanzane marinate . . . linguine and tagliatelle, both prepared with a choice of savory sauces, are recommended.

Dinner: Tues.-Sun.	Reservations Advised
Price: Moderate to Expensive	Cards: MC, V(BA)
Full Bar	Street Parking

SWISS LOUIS   (415) 421-2913
493 Broadway
    (at Kearny)
North Beach, San Francisco

    The complete robust Italian dinner at its best — generous antipasto, salad with Bay shrimp, real soup, appetizing entrees, fresh fruit and nuts. Very popular for lunch and dinner.

Dinner: Mon.-Sat.	Reservations for Sure
Lunch: Mon.-Fri.	Major Cards
Price: Moderate	Self Parking
Full Bar	

VANESSI'S   (415) 421-0890
498 Broadway
    (at Kearny)
San Francisco

    San Francisco's most versatile restaurant. From a light meal at the counter to a multi-course dinner in the dining room . . . from an early lunch to an after-midnight supper . . . from inexpensive pasta to expensive steaks and lobster. The menu is enormous with many a la carte selections. Always bustling with activity. An original.

Dinner: Every Night	Reservations Always
Lunch: Mon.-Sat.	Major Cards
Lower Priced to Expensive	Street Parking
Full Bar	

TOP TEN CONTINENTAL RESTAURANTS OF THE SAN FRANCISCO BAY AREA

BLUE FOX — (415) 981-1177
659 Merchant St.
(between Montgomery and Kearny)
Financial District, San Francisco

Blue Fox evokes nostalgia...and as time passes it continues to be one of the city's better restaurants. While the menu is Continental, the accent is Italian. Superb pastas (tortellini alla Veneziana is recommended), large selection of chicken, veal and beef dishes.

Dinner: Mon.-Sat.   Reservations Necessary
Price: Expensive to Very   Major Cards
Full Bar   Valet Parking
                            Jacket and Tie Requested

LE CLUB — (415) 771-5400
1250 Jones St.
(in Clay-Jones Apt.)
Nob Hill, San Francisco

This tiny restaurant is not a club at all, but a very public place. It is intimate and formal. Quite chic — but it is public. Beef Cendrillon, sweetbreads with mushrooms and truffles, and excellent veal dishes are featured. Make a reservation and you'll receive personalized matches.

Dinner: Mon.-Sat.   Reservations Vital
Price: Expensive to Very   Major Cards
Full Bar   Valet Parking
                            Jacket and Tie Requested

FOURNOU'S OVENS — (415) 989-1910
Stanford Court Hotel
905 California St.
Nob Hill, San Francisco
See "Top Ten Restaurants of San Francisco," page 65.

LA HACIENDA — (408) 354-6669
18840 Saratoga-Los Gatos Rd.
(on Highway 9)
Los Gatos

To our knowledge, this is the only Continental/Italian restaurant in a former Japanese Tea House with a Mexican name

75

in California. The building dates back to 1883. Today the menu combines Continental, Italian and American dishes. Complete dinners.

Dinner and Lunch Daily   Reservations Vital
Price: Moderate to Expensive   Major Cards
Full Bar   Big Parking Lot

NARSAI'S   (415) 527-7900
385 Colusa
(North of Berkeley)
Kensington
See "Top Ten Restaurants of San Francisco," page 66.

NORMAN'S   (415) 655-5291
3204 College
(at Alcatraz)
Berkeley
Nice wood tones and soft lights make you feel good. Relaxed. The kind of place you can take your wife, children, client or girl friend. Some popular entrees: chicken curry with homemade chutney, calves liver with onions, roast beef blintzes. Consistently good.

Dinner: Every Night   Reservations Recommended
Lunch: Mon.-Fri.   Major Cards
Price: Moderate   Street Parking
Full Bar

ROLF'S   (415) 673-8881
757 Beach
(near Fisherman's Wharf)
San Francisco
Rolf's is an intimate oasis in the hectic Ghirardelli/Cannery/Fisherman's Wharf area where you can enjoy honest cocktails and good food. Also a dandy view of the Bay, Marin, Alcatraz and Golden Gate Bridge. Fine wine list.

Dinner & Lunch: Tues.-Sun.   Reservations Accepted
Brunch: Sun., 10-3   Major Cards
Price: Moderate to Expensive   Parking in Rear
Full Bar

SOUPCON   (415) 332-9752
49 Caledonia St.
Sausalito

This miniscule restaurant serves some of the best soups, sandwiches and salads anywhere. Soups are originals: chicken and avocado; spinach and oyster; blackbean, rum and banana. Dinner entrees include fresh fish, chicken with avocado and cheese, steak Dijon. Good for dinner, even better for lunch.

Dinner & Lunch: Every Day	Reservations Essential
Price: Moderate	No Cards
Wine and Beer	Self Parking

SWISS CELLAR   (415) 461-5566
9 Ross Commons
Ross

French, Italian and German-Swiss dishes are featured in this inviting little candlelit restaurant tucked into a store-front location. Skillful preparation of veal, chicken, rack of lamb and duck. Owners will make you feel warm and welcome.

Dinner: Tues.-Sun.	Reservations Advised
Lunch: Tues.-Fri.	Cards: MC, V(BA)
Price: Moderate	Street Parking
Wine and Beer	

TRADER VIC'S   (415) 653-3400
9 Anchor Drive
Watergate Complex
Emeryville
See "Top Ten Restaurants of San Francisco," Page 67.

TOP TEN RESTAURANTS FOR STEAK, CHICKEN, GUMBO AND OTHER AMERICAN FAVORITES IN THE SAN FRANCISCO BAY AREA

THE BEGINNING — (415) 563-9948
2020 Fillmore
(near California)
San Francisco

There is an American cuisine, and The Beginning is where you'll find it: ham hocks, gumbo, southern fried chicken, breaded pork chops and such delectables. All-American desserts: sweet potato pie, peach or blackberry cobbler. The owner is basketball star Nate Thurmond. No wonder he grew so big.

Dinner & Lunch: Tues.-Sun.   Reservations: 5 or more
Price: Moderate   No Credit Cards
Full Bar   Street Parking

CANLIS' — (415) 392-0113
Fairmont Hotel
California at Mason Sts.
Nob Hill, San Francisco

Kimono-clad Japanese waitresses serve outstanding seafood, steaks and chops in a sophisticated Hawaiian atmosphere. Meats are expertly broiled over Hawaiian Keawewood Charcoal. Chic.

Dinner: Mon.-Sat.   Reservations Recommended
Price: Moderate to Expensive   Major Cards
Full Bar   Valet Parking
    Jackets Required

LE CREOLE — (415) 921-1132
1809 Union St.
(near Octavia)
Cow Hollow, San Francisco

Gumbos, jambalaya, pecan pie and bread and whiskey pudding are all taste treats at this Louisiana-style restaurant whose advice for hungry diners is, "Gumbo gladdens the stomach while it soothes the soul." What more can you ask?

Dinner: Every Night   Reservations Recommended
Lunch: Mon.-Sat.   Major Cards
Lower Priced to Moderate   Self Parking

Wine and Beer

THE ELEGANT FARMER   (415) 893-5292
34 Jack London Square
Oakland

Bring a big appetite! Just good food, and lots of it, at reasonable prices. Prime rib. Steaks. Lobster tails. Fried chicken.
Roast leg of lamb. Family dinners on Sunday. American favorites, all!

Dinner: Every Night	Reservations Advised
Lunch: Mon.-Fri.	Major Cards
Price: Moderate	Valet and Self Parking
Full Bar	

GRISON'S   (415) 673-1888
2100 Van Ness Avenue
  (at Pacific)
Downtown, San Francisco

This old-time San Francisco restaurant still has some of the
best steaks in town. What's more, excellent prime rib is served
from carts at tableside. Grison's Caesar salad is a good way
to start.

Dinner: Wed.-Mon.	Reservations: 6 or more
(closed Tuesday)	Major Cards
Price: Moderate to Expensive	Validated Parking
Full Bar	

GULLIVER'S   (415) 692-6060
1699 Old Bayshore
  (near San Francisco Airport)
Burlingame

At dinner, Gulliver's serves excellent prime rib, and only
prime rib, in your choice of cuts. With spinach, fresh vegetables, salad or soup. At lunch, chicken pot pie, hash, fish and
chips and beef dishes are featured. Decor is laden with Gulliver
artifacts. Attentive "wench and squire" service.

Dinner: Every Night	Reservations for Sure
Lunch: Mon.-Fri.	Cards: MC, V(BA)
Price: Moderate	Parking Lot
Full Bar	

Other Locations:
Marina del Rey (Los Angeles); Irvine (Orange County)

THE IRON WORKS   (415) 493-3433
3877 El Camino Real
  (south of University Avenue)
Palo Alto

The Iron Works identifies its food as early-California.   79

Actually, it's a combination of American with picturesque names (Miner's Bones, Sutter Stew, Gold Rush sandwich), Mexican (chili rellenos, enchiladas) and steaks. Champagne brunch. Covered outdoor patio.

Dinner: Every Night	Reservations: 5 or more
Lunch: Mon.-Fri.	Cards: AE, MC, V(BA)
Brunch: Sun., 10:30-2:30	Parking in Rear
Price: Moderate	
Wine and Beer	

THE LEOPARD   (415) 392-3348
140 Front St.
(near California)
Financial District, San Francisco

Known for big drinks, huge steaks, double-cut pork or lamb chops, fresh salads and baked potatoes. This plain looking place attracts he-man appetites. Ladies and kids are welcome too, (child's plates).

Dinner & Lunch: Mon.-Sat.	Reservations Accepted
Price: Moderate	Major Cards
Full Bar	Self Parking

MacARTHUR PARK   (415) 398-5700
607 Front St.
(between Pacific & Jackson)
Financial District, San Francisco

This restaurant is in an old warehouse, transformed into an indoor park ... complete with trees, plants, water and aviary. Lots of steaks plus chops, rack of lamb, prime rib, duckling, chicken and seafood. Good salads and homemade soups. Particularly popular at lunch. Outstanding selection of California wines.

Dinner: Every Night	Reservations: Dinner Only
Lunch: Mon.-Fri.	Cards: AE, MC, V(BA)
Sunday Brunch: 10:30-2:30	Valet Parking
Price: Moderate	
Full Bar	

MAMA'S

Washington Square	(415) 362-6421
Union Square (Macy's)	(415) 391-3790
Nob Hill (Grovesnor Towers)	(415) 928-1004
San Mateo (Macy's)	(415) 573-1176

See "Top Ten Restaurants of California," Pages 26-27.

TOP TEN SEAFOOD RESTAURANTS OF
THE SAN FRANCISCO BAY AREA

THE MAST   (415) 465-2188
75 Jack London Square
Oakland
Spectacular natural-wood and glass architecture provides
yacht basin view. A beautiful setting for well prepared and
attractively presented seafood dishes.

Dinner & Lunch: Tues.-Sun.	Reservations Advised
Price: Moderate	Major Cards
Full Bar	Parking Lot

THE PACIFIC CAFE   (415) 387-7091
7000 Geary Blvd.
  (at 34th)
Richmond District, San Francisco
This is the original of what has quickly grown to a three
restaurant chain featuring a short but varied list of seafood.
Turbot stuffed with crab and shrimp, then baked in parchment.
Petrale sole. Halibut. Salmon. Pan fried oysters. Terrific french
fries. Bring the family.

Dinner: Every Night	No Reservations
Price: Moderate	No Credit Cards
Wine and Beer	Self Parking

Other Locations:

Ghirardelli Square   **(415) 775-1173**
900 N. Point   Cards: AE, MC, V(BA)
San Francisco   Validated Garage Parking
Dinner and Lunch Daily
Full Bar

850 College Ave.   **(415) 456-3898**
Kentfield (Marin Co.)   No Reservations
Dinner: Tues.-Sun.   No Credit Cards
Wine and Beer

POMPEI'S GROTTO   (415) 776-9265
Fisherman's Wharf
340 Jefferson St.
San Francisco
No view, but we find the seafood is the best on Fisherman's
Wharf. Lots of broiled, grilled and poached fish and seafood.

Some of the tastiest dishes are Italian-style. Try the fresh Dungeness crab — or an order of "steamers."

Dinner and Lunch Daily	Reservations Advised
Price: Moderate	Major Cards
Full Bar	Self Parking

SAM'S GRILL   (415) 421-0594
374 Bush St.
(between Kearny and Montgomery)
Financial District, San Francisco

Sam's is one of San Francisco's great old-time restaurants, and while it's best known for superb seafood, Sam's menu is much broader, with excellent veal, chicken, beef and egg dishes. But seafood is the star (our favorite is Sand Dabs ala Sam). Open from 11:30 a.m. to 8:30 p.m.

Dinner & Lunch: Mon.-Fri.	Reservations: 6 or more
Price: Moderate	Cards: MC, V(BA)
Full Bar	Self Parking

SCOTT'S SEAFOOD GRILL AND BAR
2400 Lombard St.   (415) 567-7725
(at Scott)
Marina District, San Francisco

Scott's is new and fast becoming a famous local seafood house. Informal furnishings, wood and tiles — an old San Francisco look. Menu is mostly a la carte, but there is also a good three-course dinner.

Dinner & Lunch: Every Day	No Reservations
Price: Moderate	Cards: AE, MC, V(BA)
Full Bar	Valet Parking

SEVEN SEAS   (415) 982-8833
682 Bridgeway
Sausalito

A tempting menu (red snapper creole, crab and shrimp omelette, mahi mahi, petrale sole), sensible prices, outdoor dining, a fun place. Popular in Marin County. Close to the ferry terminal — on a bright day, cruise over and enjoy.

Dinner and Lunch Daily	No Reservations
Price: Moderate	Cards: AE, MC, V(BA)
Full Bar	Parking Lot

SPENGER'S FISH GROTTO   (415) 845-7771
1919 4th St.
  (off University)
Berkeley

We've heard that this enormous restaurant serves more dinners than any other in the west. What's remarkable is the standard they maintain — consistently top quality seafood at very reasonable prices. The menu is also enormous — about 75 entrees. So popular, waits are usually long.

Open 8 a.m. to Midnight   Reservations: 6 or more
   Every Day   Major Cards
Lower Priced to Moderate   Big Parking Lot
Full Bar
Children's Plates

SWAN OYSTER DEPOT   (415) 673-1101
1517 Polk St.
  (near California)
Downtown San Francisco

Combination fish market and oyster bar. Excellent cracked crabs, oyster and shrimp cocktails, clams, seafood salads and New England chowder are served from the 18-seat marble counter.

Open: Mon.-Sat.,   No Reservations
   (8 a.m. to 5:30 p.m.)   No Cards
Price: Moderate   Self Parking
Wine and Beer

Other Recommended Seafood Bars:
Bogart's—A Shellfish Bar   (415) 397-0233
661 Clay   Mon.-Sat., 10 a.m.-3:30 p.m.
  (at Kearny)
Financial District, San Francisco

Bogart's   **(415) 922-9370**
2066 Union   Daily: 11 a.m. to Midnight
Cow Hollow, San Francisco

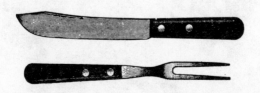

TADICH GRILL

(415) 391-2373

240 California St.
Financial District, San Francisco
See "Top Ten Restaurants of California," Pages 20-21.

THE WATERFRONT

(415) 391-2696

Pier 7, Embarcadero
**   (at Broadway)**
San Francisco

Attractive new restaurant in an old, renovated waterfront building. Lively view of San Francisco Bay activity. Seafood is the specialty but steaks and pasta are also on the menu. Nice for cocktails or brunch.

Dinner: Every Night
Lunch: Mon.-Fri.
Brunch: Sat., Sun., 11-3
Price: Moderate
Full Bar

Reservations Recommended
Cards: AE, MC, V(BA)
Valet Parking

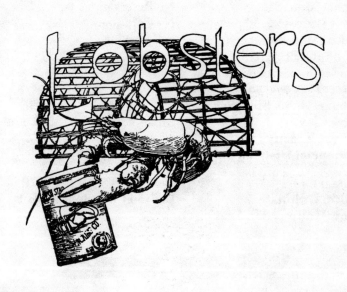

TOP TEN ORIENTAL RESTAURANTS OF THE SAN FRANCISCO BAY AREA

THE CHERRY FLOWER (Vietnamese)
124 Columbus Ave.   **(415) 398-9101**
  (near Jackson)
North Beach, San Francisco   ·

Vietnamese specialties include roast crab, Pho (a soup with noodles, strips of beef and spices), shrimp balls, brochette de porc. Excellent and different—courteous service and traditional Southeast Asian atmosphere.

Dinner: Tues.-Sun.	Reservations Advisable
Lunch: Tues.-Fri.	Cards: MC, V(BA)
Lower Priced to Moderate	Street Parking
Wine and Beer	

CHINA STATION (Cantonese)   (415) 548-7880
700 University Ave.
  (in the old S.P. Depot)
Berkeley

The design is California-mission-depot-modern. An extensive Cantonese menu. The chef creates unusual Chinese seafood dishes. Large and informal, this is a good place for kids to learn their chopsticks.

Dinner and Lunch Daily	Reservations Suggested
Price: Moderate	Cards: AE, MC, V(BA)
Full Bar	Parking Lot

KEE JOON'S (Chinese)   **(415) 348-1122**
433 Airport Blvd.
Burlingame

Kee Joon's overlooks the bay and the airport. Its Oriental Sung Dynasty beauty is enhanced by an aviary and garden. The varied menu includes the cuisines of Canton, Peking and Szechuan — prepared with creativity and care.

Dinner: Every Night	Reservations Advised
Lunch: Mon.-Fri.	Cards: AE, MC, V(BA)
Price: Moderate to Expensive	Parking Lot
Full Bar/Music Weekends	

KICHIHEI (Japanese)   (415) 929-1670
2084 Chestnut
(at Steiner)
Marina District, San Francisco

Distinguished Japanese food. Experiment with dishes like salmon shioyaki, baked eggplant and shabu-shabu. Or select from nabemono — vegetables, thin noodles and tofu in broth. Excellent tempura, sashimi and sukiyaki at modest prices.

Dinner: Thurs.-Tues.	Reservations Definitely
Lunch: Mon., Tues., Thurs.-	Major Cards
Sat. (closed Wed.)	Self Parking
Lower Priced to Moderate	
Sake, Wine, Beer	

THE MANDARIN (Northern Chinese)
Ghirardelli Square   (415) 673-8812
North Point St.
San Francisco

The luxurious interior is decorated with tiles, carved screens and Chinese artifacts. Gracious owner Cecilia Chang supervises every detail. Northern Chinese dishes are on the elaborate menu. We like the "Mongolian Fire Pit," available at dinner and lunch. And there's a great view.

Dinner and Lunch Daily	Reservations Accepted
Price: Moderate to Expensive	Major Cards
Full Bar	Parking in Ghirardelli Garage

NAM YUEN (Cantonese)   (415) 781-5636
740 Washington
(between Grant and Kearny)
Chinatown, San Francisco

The Cantonese food in this lively restaurant is exceptional. Three complete dinners are on the menu, including the Chef's Masterpiece — his choice of his best dishes of the day. A la carte items from standard Chinese to exotic. Children's prices.

Dinner & Lunch: Tues.-Sun.	Reservations: 8 or more
Price: Moderate	No Cards
Full Bar	Self Parking

NORTH CHINA RESTAURANT (Mandarin)
2315 Van Ness Ave.   **(415) 673-8201**
   (at Vallejo)
San Francisco

Very popular with fans of authentic Mandarin food. The limited menu offers an easy introduction for those less familiar with this cuisine. Smoked tea duck and kung-pao shrimp are winners. Don't miss the hot and sour or sizzling rice soup. Menu and prices are the same at both locations.

Dinner & Lunch: Mon.-Sat.   Reservations Advised
Lower Priced to Moderate   No Cards
Wine and Beer   Self Parking

Other Location:
531 Jackson   **(415) 982-1708**
   (at Columbus)
North Beach, San Francisco

TAO TAO CAFE (Cantonese)   (408) 736-3731
175 So. Murphy Ave.
Sunnyvale

Friendly proprietor Frank Wong and good Cantonese food make this neighborhood restaurant special in the San Jose area. The decor isn't impressive, but the kitchen is. Our favorites are Chinese chicken salad, Tao Tao beef and orange peel duck. Call and check on special order dishes.

Dinner: Every Night   Reservations Accepted
Lunch: Mon.-Fri.   Cards: AE, MC, V (BA)
Price: Moderate   Parking in Rear
Full Bar

YANK SING (Deem Sum)   **(415) 781-1111**
671 Broadway
  (near Stockton)
North Beach, San Francisco

Deem sum (or dim sum) is a Chinese tea lunch and an old Cantonese custom. Deem sum means "little gem", and indeed they are. Saucers of plump dumplings and delicacies in great variety are brought to the table on large trays. You select what looks good. They all do! Take it easy on the first offering... lots more are coming.

Open Daily: 10AM-5PM	No Reservations
Lower Priced	No Credit Cards
Beer	Self Parking

Other Location: **(415) 495-4510**
53 Stevenson St.   No Reservations
San Francisco
Open Daily: 11AM-3PM

Another recommended restaurant for "deem sum":
ASIA GARDEN   **(415) 398-5112**
772 Pacific Ave.   Open Daily, 10AM-3PM
San Francisco

YET WAH (Northern Chinese) **(415) 387-8040**
1801, 1829 and 2140 Clement St.
Richmond District, San Francisco
See "Top Ten Restaurants of the San Francisco Bay Area,"
  Page 68.

TOP TEN INTERNATIONAL RESTAURANTS OF THE SAN FRANCISCO BAY AREA

DAVOOD'S (Middle Eastern)   (415) 388-2000
22 Miller
Mill Valley

Middle Eastern foods served in a stunning setting of redwood, stained glass, natural light and lush plants. An array of delicious curries, casseroles, kababs, dolmas, and seafood. Homemade bread, soups and desserts. Provocative luncheon menu.

Dinner and Lunch Daily   Reservations Advised
Price: Moderate to Expensive Cards: AE, MC, V(BA)
Wine and Beer   Parking Lot

EMILE'S SWISS AFFAIR (Swiss)
545 South Second St.   (408) 289-1960
San Jose

A chef-owned Swiss restaurant, with French accents. Enticing appetizers including quenelles nantua, pate and fettuccini Alfredo. Lamb, beef, prawns and veal prepared with superb sauces. Complete dinners are the best buy.

Dinner: Tues.-Sun.   Reservations Advised
Price: Moderate to Expensive Cards: AE, MC, V(BA)
Wine and Beer   Parking Lot

GAYLORD (Indian)   (415) 771-8822
Ghirardelli Square
900 N. Point St.
San Francisco

Sip a Pimm's cup and relax overlooking the Bay. Gaylord's lunch and dinner specialty is tandoor cookery...a technique using clay ovens to cook marinated chicken, lamb and fish. Several Indian curries. Dine in a room filled with plump pillows and Indian decorations.

Dinner and Lunch Daily   Reservations Recommended
Price: Moderate to Expensive Cards: AE, MC, V(BA)
Full Bar   Validation for Parking Garage

LOVE'S PAGAN'S DEN (Philippine)
760 East 8th St.   (415) 832-3383
Oakland

Good Philippine cooking is difficult to find until you discover the Pagan's Den. For example: tiger prawns in coconut milk and ginger, crab in black bean sauce, chorizo-stuffed game hen. Polynesian food for the less adventurous. Chef Ben Love and brother Art have created a super little place.

Dinner: Tues.-Sun.	Reservations Advised
Lunch: Tues.-Fri.	Cards: MC, V(BA)
Lower Priced to Moderate	Parking Lot in Rear
Full Bar	

EL MANSOUR (Moroccan)   (415) 731-2312
3123 Clement St.
Richmond Dist., San Francisco

A unique dining experience, not for everyone. Be prepared to eat with your fingers...no utensils here. A multi-course meal features harira (lentil soup), salad, bastilla (a concoction of pastry, chicken, spices and nuts). Large choice of dishes include couscous, turkey with almonds and lamb. The dessert — friend bananas with honey, and mint tea.

Dinner: Tues.-Sun.	Reservations Recommended
Price: Moderate	Cards: MC, V(BA)
Wine	Street Parking

MONROE'S (English)   (415) 567-4550
1968 Lombard
(near Webster)
Marina Dist., San Francisco

A restaurant that could have been transported directly from England. The menu is limited, but all done nicely. Recommended are mushroom salad, beef brochette bernaise, grenadin of veal, prime rib with Yorkshire pudding. Quite English, tipsy trifle for dessert.

Dinner: Tues.-Sun.	Reservations Advised
Price: Moderate	Cards: MC, V(BA)
Full Bar	Street Parking

PAPRIKA'S FONO (Hungarian)
Ghirardelli Square   (415) 441-1223
900 North Point St.
San Francisco

Inside, Paprika's Fono resembles a rustic country inn. Outside offers terrace dining with a view. Authentic Hungarian food. We like the gulyas, broth with chunks of beef and potatoes, chicken paprikas, and Mother's palacsintak — pancakes with a variety of fillings. Accompany them with Hungarian wine.

Dinner and Lunch Daily	Reservations Recommended
Price: Moderate	Cards: MC, V (BA)
Full Bar	Parking Ghirardelli Garage

EL TOREADOR (Mexican)   (415) 664-9800
50 West Portal Ave.
(near Vicente)
Sunset Dist., San Francisco

Authentic Mexican cooking, as well as the more familiar tacos, frijoles and tamales. Chicken mole, enchilada with mole, and chili verde are all bueno! South-of-the-border feel with lots of tiles and wrought iron in this neighborhood favorite.

Dinner: Every Night	Reservations Accepted
Lunch: Mon.-Fri.	Cards: MC, V (BA)
Lower Priced	Street Parking
Wine and Beer	

TYCOON (Eastern Mediterranean)
4012 Geary Blvd.   (415) 387-9600
(near 5th Avenue)
Richmond Dist., San Francisco

The imaginative Vartan brothers created this handsome restaurant — inspired by the idea that guests should feel like tycoons. Enjoy Eastern Mediterranean dishes like Chicken Sevan and Koufta a la Ourpha (ground lamb with cracked wheat). Dinners start with Phoenician appetizers, pita bread and soup. Bourma (baklava) for dessert.

Dinner: Wed.-Mon.	Reservations Accepted
(closed Tues.)	No Credit Cards
Price: Moderate	Street Parking
Wine and Beer	

VLASTA'S EUROPEAN INN (Czechoslovakian)
2420 Lombard St.   (415) 931-7533
(near Scott)
Marina Dist., San Francisco

A popular family place. Lots of Czech and Hungarian food. Generous portions of roast duck with dumplings, goulash, roast pork and stuffed cabbage. Dinners with rich soup and salad. If you can manage it, there's a flaky apple strudel.

Dinner: Tues.-Sun.	Reservations Advised
Price: Moderate	Cards: MC, V (BA)
Full Bar	Street Parking

TOP TEN SOUP, SALAD, SANDWICH, SNACK AND SUPPER RESTAURANTS OF THE SAN FRANCISCO BAY AREA

BILL'S PLACE   (415) 221-5262
2315 Clement St.
   (near 24th Avenue)
Richmond Dist., San Francisco

Bill's Place is a San Francisco institution with first-rate hamburgers. Service indoors or on the garden patio. Bill's also has chili, hot dogs, Polish sausage, lots of sandwiches and good desserts. Well-behaved kids are welcome.

Dinner and Lunch Daily	No Reservations
Lower Priced	No Credit Cards
No Liquor	Parking Lot — daytime only — ½-block on Clement

Other Location:
GET Shopping Mall   **(415) 566-1146**
Sloat Blvd. at 34th Avenue   Open Daily
San Francisco

BRENNAN'S   (415) 841-0960
720 University Ave.
Berkeley

Brennan's is good for tasty rib-sticking food in large portions at low prices. Great turkey, beef and corned beef are sliced to order and served hot or cold. Regular dishes include chow mein, chowder and giant turkey legs. A big island bar sells generous drinks.

Dinner & Lunch: Mon.-Sat.	No Reservations
Lower Priced	No Credit Cards
Full Bar	Parking Lot

THE BROKEN EGG OMELET HOUSE
340 No. Santa Cruz Ave.   **(408) 354-2554**
Los Gatos

An inviting place for breakfast, lunch or a light dinner. A natural for omelet buffs. Choose from fruit, cheese, meat, vegetable or seafood — or create your own combination. Forget calories and indulge in a healthy fruit shake.

Daily: 7AM-11PM	No Reservations
(same menu all day)	No Credit Cards
Lower Priced / No Liquor	Self Parking

Other Locations:

605 Front   **(408) 426-0157**
Santa Cruz

Mission & 5th Avenue   **(408) 625-1904**
Carmel

CAFFE SPORT   **(415) 981-1251**
574 Green St.
   (near Stockton)
North Beach, San Francisco
    Caffe Sport is very unique, very small and very Italian.
Every inch was built and decorated by owner Antonio La
Tona. Special sandwiches of Italian cold cuts and cheeses —
deliciously sauced pastas and seafoods. Stop in for Capuccino.

Dinner & Lunch: Mon.-Sat.	No Reservations
Lower Priced to Moderate	No Credit Cards
Wine and Beer	Self Parking (good luck)

CARAVANSARY   **(415) 362-4640**
310 Sutter St.
   (near Grant)
Downtown San Francisco
    Caravansary is both a gourmet retail store and a restaurant.
Enter the second floor restaurant through a separate door. At
lunchtime try Aram's sandwich — roast beef, cream cheese and
pickled cucumber — a splendid quiche, or chef's original salad.
Armenian-style dishes for dinner and lunch.

Dinner & Lunch: Mon.-Sat.	Reservations Dinner Only
Price: Moderate	Cards: AE, MC, V(BA)
Full Bar	Self Parking

Another Location:

2263 Chestnut St.   **(415) 921-3466**
Marina District,   Reservations Dinner Only
   San Francisco   Street Parking

THE GARRET   **(408) 371-6505**
The Prune Yard
Campbell (San Jose area)
    Climb up to the Garret and have one of their great, *grilled*
hamburgers, fries and a crispy salad. Large sandwich menu.
Huge assortment of beer. Self-service only. Informal and fun.

Dinner and Lunch Daily	No Reservations
Lower Priced	No Credit Cards
Wine and Beer	

PAM PAM EAST   (415) 433-0113
398 Geary
(in the Raphael Hotel)
Downtown San Francisco

Twenty-four hours a day this is a superior "coffee shop." Thick slices of French toast, fluffy waffles, egg dishes and soup are always available. Good family place.

Open 24 hours daily	No Reservations
Lower Priced to Moderate	Major Cards
Full Bar	Self Parking

LA QUICHE   (415) 441-2711
550 Taylor St.
(between Post and Geary)
Downtown San Francisco

Small, neat, informal, friendly, very French. Thirty-eight a la carte crepes. Quiche Lorraine is the house specialty.

Dinner and Lunch Daily	No Reservations
Lower Priced to Moderate	Cards: MC, V(BA)
Wine and Beer	Self Parking

SEARS' FINE FOOD   (415) 986-1160
439 Powell St.
(between Post and Sutter)
Downtown San Francisco

A San Francisco landmark, serving American food at reasonable prices. From an extensive menu, choose waffles, artichokes, banana bread or roast turkey. Fine for early meals.

Daily: 7AM-3PM	Reservations: 6 or more
Lower Priced	No Credit Cards
No Liquor	Self Parking

WHAT THIS COUNTRY NEEDS
Hyatt Hotel-Union Square   (415) 982-4280
San Francisco

Tasty homemade soups and sandwiches served cafeteria-style. Three different soups available daily — such as Cuban blackbean, puree of zucchini and Greek Avgolemono.

Dinner & Lunch: Mon.-Sat.	No Reservations
Lower Priced	No Credit Cards
Wine and Beer	Self Parking

Other Location:
1st and Market   **(415) 495-9466**
San Francisco   Full Bar

TOP TEN GOOD DEAL RESTAURANTS OF THE SAN FRANCISCO BAY AREA

CAFE BIARRITZ   **(415) 982-0751**
391 Broadway
  (at Montgomery)
North Beach, San Francisco

A bar-restaurant with family-style food and prices. Table d'hote dinners change nightly, include soup, entree, salad, dessert and coffee. Basque-style cooking. Good Coquilles St. Jacques and rack of lamb.

Dinner and Lunch:	Reservations Recommended
Tues.-Sun.	Cards: CB, MC, V(BA)
Brunch: Sun., 11-3	Valet Parking
Price: Moderate	
Full Bar	

CHEZ LEON   **(415) 982-1093**
124 Ellis St.
  (between Mason and Powell)
Downtown San Francisco

Nice things happen here. Complimentary Champagne at Saturday lunch, and roses for the ladies. Service and food are tops. A daily special and the complete dinners make this a "good deal."

Dinner & Lunch: Tues.-Sat.	Reservations Advised
Price: Moderate	Major Cards
Full Bar	Self Parking

THE COACHMAN   **(415) 362-1696**
1057 Powell St.
  (at Washington)
Downtown San Francisco

English decor, friendly service and reliable food. Lots of a la carte dishes, but the best buy is the special dinner. House specialties are steak and kidney pie, salmon (in season) or top sirloin. Choice of salad or cockie-leekie soup. Cheerio!

Dinner: Every Night	Reservations for Sure
Price: Moderate	Major Cards
Full Bar	Valet Parking

THE GOLDEN EAGLE   (415) 982-8831
160 California St.
(at Front)
Financial Dist., San Francisco

The Golden Eagle feeds you well and makes you welcome. It does a roaring lunch business. And dinners are complete — including unusual soup, salad and neat desserts. Try chicken San Joaquin, beef vinaigrette, hunter's stew.

Dinner & Lunch: Mon.-Fri.	Reservations for Sure at Lunch
Price: Moderate	Cards: AE, MC, V(BA)
Full Bar	Self Parking

OUI FONDUE   (415) 752-3003
2435 Clement St.
Richmond Dist., San Francisco

For something different, inexpensive and informal a favorite is Oui Fondue. Try a rich cheese fondue or the beef fondue with assorted sauces. Add a chilled glass of wine or frosty beer.

Dinner: Every Night	Reservations Accepted
Price: Moderate	Cards: MC, V(BA)
Wine and Beer	Self Parking

LA PANTERA   (415) 392-0170
1234 Grant Ave.
North Beach, San Francisco

An amiable North Beach restaurant serving family style multi-course meals. No choices here. Homemade soup is followed with pasta and tongue Pomidoro, then a platter of meat or fish, salad, fruit and cheese.

Dinner: Tues.-Sun.	No Reservations
Lunch: Tues.-Fri.	No Credit Cards
Price: Moderate	Street Parking
Full Bar	

SCHROEDER'S   (415) 421-4778
240 Front St.
(near California)
Financial Dist., San Francisco

German food has been enjoyed in this large, masculine restaurant since 1893. Now *"Ladies* and Gentlemen" are invited for lunch and dinner. Blackboard menus feature German dishes — plus entrees like shrimp curry and fried oysters.

Dinner & Lunch: Mon.-Fri.	Reservations Accepted
Lower Priced to Moderate	No Credit Cards
Full Bar	Validated Parking for Dinner

TOMMASO'S   (415) 398-9696
1042 Kearny
(near Broadway)
North Beach, San Francisco

Pizza baked in an oak burning oven...plus Neopolitan style cooking are featured in this long established restaurant. Some unique salads such as sweet peppers, broccoli and zucchini. A good selection of pasta, veal and chicken.

Dinner: Wed.-Sun.	No Reservations
Price: Moderate	Cards: MC, V(BA)
Wine and Beer	Self Parking

UPSTART CROW AND COMPANY
The Prune Yard   (408) 371-5743
Campbell (San Jose area)

A bookstore, restaurant and coffee house. Salads, sandwiches, quiche. Entrees from chicken Marengo to pot roast. Some children's portions. Live chamber music is served with the Champagne Brunch.

Dinner and Lunch Daily	Reservations Accepted
Brunch: Sun., 10-2:30	Major Cards
Lower Priced to Moderate	Parking Lot
Wine and Beer	

THE WIDOW AND PANCHO VILLA
470 Pacific Ave.   (415) 392-5630
(near Montgomery)
Financial Dist., San Francisco

Spicy Tex-Mex items prepared in a superior kitchen. Hot chili. The Widow also entices with more off beat items—chicken mole, chimichanga (translation on menu). Child's plates... attractive...Ole!

Dinner: Every Night	Reservations Accepted
Lunch: Mon.-Fri.	Cards: MC, V(BA)
Lower Priced to Moderate	Self Parking
Full Bar	

TOP TEN SPECIAL INTEREST RESTAURANTS OF THE SAN FRANCISCO BAY AREA

THE BUENA VISTA   (415) 474-5044
2765 Hyde St. (at Beach)
Near Fisherman's Wharf
San Francisco

While this historic restaurant dates back to 1899, it was its introduction of Irish coffee to the U.S. in 1953 which gives The Buena Vista its current notoriety. San Franciscan's prefer it for its huge breakfasts which are served from 9AM to 9:30PM. Also sandwiches and light meals. Always crowded.

Dinner, Lunch,	No Reservations
Breakfast: Daily	No Credit Cards
Lower Priced	Self Parking
Full Bar (Very Full)	

THE CANNERY   (415) 771-3112
2801 Leavenworth   (for information)
Near Fisherman's Wharf
San Francisco

Walk, browse, watch street musicians and mimes, shop or eat in this converted Del Monte cannery that dates back to the 19th century. Many pleasant eating places including Ben Jonson, El Sombrero, Old Brittany, Shang Yuen and Crivello's Oyster Bar plus the superb Cannery Gourmet and Wine Cellars. Open 7 days, but hours vary by establishment.

CARNELIAN ROOM   (415) 433-7500
Bank of America Bldg.
555 California
    (at Montgomery)
Financial Dist., San Francisco

From the 52nd floor of the Bank of America Building, the Carnelian Room offers San Francisco's top view... the Golden Gate, the Bay, the hills of Marin and the city below. Spectacular. But the Carnelian Room offers even more... it's also a handsome restaurant with a Continental menu. Seafood, veal and beef are featured. Two table d'hote dinners plus extensive a la carte menu.

Dinner: Every Night	Reservations Essential
Brunch: Sun., 10-3	Major Cards
Price: Expensive to Very	Validated Parking
Full Bar	

DOMAINE CHANDON   (707) 944-2467
California Drive
Yountville, Napa Valley

Domaine Chandon is one of California's newer wineries, producing sparkling wines in the tradition of its parent, Moet and Chandon. In April, 1977 they started public tours, demonstrating all the steps of the "methode champenoise." In June, they opened their French restaurant featuring an elegant buffet at lunch time and formal dining in the evening. Fresh fish, duckling, rack of lamb and Domaine Chandon's sparkling wines are featured.

Dinner and Lunch:
   Thurs.-Mon.
Price: Expensive
Domaine Chandon Wines
Visitor's Center Open
   11AM-5:30PM, Thurs.-
   Mon. (Closed Tues.-Wed.)

Reservations Vital (Weekends,
   well in Advance)
Cards: AE, MC, V(BA)
Parking Lot

FISHERMAN'S WHARF

Crowded, noisy, swarming with pitchmen hawking souvenirs...yet wonderful. That's Fisherman's Wharf, one of the most colorful spots in San Francisco, or anywhere. Enjoy a shrimp or crabmeat sidewalk cocktail. Or, in season, fresh steamed Dungeness crab. Pompei's Grotto has the best food on the wharf, but there's no view. So if you're planning lunch or dinner, look first...then eat.

GHIRARDELLI SQUARE   (415) 775-5500
Beach at Larkin   **(for information)**
San Francisco

This converted chocolate factory originally built in 1893 houses some of San Francisco's best restaurants plus interesting shops and one of the world's classic views — across the bay to the soaring Golden Gate Bridge. You'll find many of Ghirardelli's restaurants detailed elsewhere in the "Top Ten Book" (Paprika's Fono, Gaylord, The Mandarin, Pacific Cafe and Modesto Lanzone). But they're just the start. Whatever you want from pastry to formal dinner, from sandwiches to ice cream sundae, you'll find it at Ghirardelli. The Square's most popular spot is the Ghirardelli Chocolate Manufactory Soda Fountain and Candy Shop. Great sodas, milk shakes and huge sundaes.

MODESTO LANZONE'S　　　(415) 771-2880
Ghirardelli Square
Beach at Larkin
San Francisco

This is not only one of the best Italian restaurants in San Francisco, but it is the perfect setting for that intimate lunch. The Loggia room is like sitting in a sheltered garden, looking out over the bay, the boats, the bridge and the distant shores of Marin. Try the Panzotti — pasta with spinach, ricotta and prosciutto topped with cream sauce and crushed walnuts. Fantastico.

Dinner: Tues.-Sun.　　　Reservations Advised
Lunch: Tues.-Fri.　　　Major Cards
Price: Expensive　　　Validated Parking in Garage
Full Bar

THE NUT TREE　　　(707) 448-6411
Interstate 80
Vacaville

Starting in 1921 as a fruit stand, The Nut Tree has emerged as the state's most "California" restaurant. The cheerful flower-filled dining room, the bountiful menu, the gift shop . . . all say "California." Fabulous fruit and vegetable salads are made with whatever is fresh. California's early Mexican and Chinese influence are represented by a superior turkey tamale and excellent stir fry dishes. Good fresh breads and outstanding desserts. Extensive list of California wines. Nut Tree is a fast 56 miles from San Francisco on the main highway to Sacramento — Interstate 80.

Dinner, Lunch, Breakfast:　　Reservations Accepted
　　Every Day　　　　　　　　(except on Sundays and
Price: Moderate　　　　　　　　Holidays)
Wine and Beer　　　　　　Cards: MC, V(BA)
　　　　　　　　　　　　　Parking Lot

THE OCCIDENTAL THREE

FIORI'S	(707) 823-8188
NEGRI'S	(707) 823-5301
THE UNION HOTEL	(707) 874-3662

Occidental (west of Santa Rosa)

Occidental is a small town that serves big Italian dinners... lots of them. It is said that on Mother's Day more than 10,000 people swarm into Occidental to dine at one of the three very similar restaurants which serve the enormous meals. The Union Hotel, which dates from 1867, is the largest. Fiori's is the smallest... and the only one which offers a varied menu. Negri's prices are slightly below the others... although all three are in the "lower price to moderate" range. Chicken, duck and steak are featured in all three... and dinners include antipasto, soup, pasta, salad, entree, dessert and coffee. All three are open daily, accept reservations, and have full bar service. Occidental is about 70 miles from San Francisco.

SABELLA'S OF MARIN   (415) 435-2636
9 Main Street
Tiburon

It is difficult to imagine a more picturesque setting than the village of Tiburon on a sunny day... its wooded hillsides jutting into San Francisco Bay and the spectacular view of the city skyline beyond. Sabella's is the newest of several waterfront restaurants which enjoy this view. Seafood is the specialty... and you can enjoy it from the glass-enclosed second story Victorian dining room or the outdoor deck which juts over the water. The Dock and Sam's Anchor Cafe are nearby and offer the same fine view.

Dinner and Lunch Daily	No Reservations
Price: Moderate	Major Cards
Full Bar	Self Parking

TOP TEN SALOONS AND OTHER GREAT PLACES FOR A DRINK IN SAN FRANCISCO

BIG FOUR   **(415) 771-1140**
Huntington Hotel
1075 California St.
Nob Hill, San Francisco
   Handsome new bar in an old-fashioned, mid-1800s tradition salutes California's "Big Four": Crocker, Huntington, Hopkins and Stanford.

REDWOOD ROOM BAR   **(415) 775-4700**
Clift Hotel
Geary at Taylor
Downtown San Francisco
   An urbane downtown bar where drinks are still mixed generously and with care.

HENRY AFRICA   **(415) 928-7044**
2260 Van Ness Ave.
San Francisco
   Convival meeting place that stays active late into the night. A conglomoration of decor including electric trains which zip about overhead.

HYATT REGENCY HOTEL ATRIUM LOBBY
Market at California   **(415) 788-1234**
Financial Dist., San Francisco
   This spectacular architectural showplace features free jazz concerts Saturday afternoon, "Big Band Tea Dancing" on Friday nights. Cocktails served in an indoor garden atmosphere.

PERRY'S   **(415) 922-9022**
1944 Union St.
Cow Hollow, San Francisco
   Probably San Francisco's most popular bar . . . lots of activity, lots of people right up to closing.

THE ROYAL EXCHANGE   (415) 956-1710
301 Sacramento
Financial Dist., San Francisco

Handsome English-style bar in the heart of San Francisco's Financial District. Popular after-work meeting place.

S. HOLMES, ESQ.   (415) 776-2100
Grovesnor Tower
1177 California St.
Nob Hill, San Francisco

San Francisco's classiest bar serves excellent drinks in a club-like atmosphere dedicated to the memory of the legendary English detective. Live piano and hot hors d'oeuvres during the cocktail hour. See Holmes' study, recreated in a private alcove.

HOUSE OF SHIELD'S   (415) 392-7732
39 New Montgomery
(So. of Market)
Downtown San Francisco

"Bar Dice" is a San Francisco tradition, and nowhere is the game played with more energy than at Shield's, a no-nonsense businessman's bar also noted for honest drinks.

SINBAD'S   (415) 781-2555
Pier 2
(So. of the Ferry Bldg.)
San Francisco

Cocktails on the San Francisco waterfront with a great view of Bay and Bridge.

VICTOR'S   (415) 956-7777
Hotel St. Francis
Powell at Geary
San Francisco

From the 32nd Floor of the Hotel St. Francis, Victor's cocktail lounge provides a magnificent view of City and Bay. Cocktails are good, service dignified.

TOP TEN RESTAURANTS OF
GREATER SAN DIEGO

ANTHONY'S FISH GROTTO   **(714) 232-5103**

**ANTHONY'S STAR OF
THE SEA ROOM**   **(714) 232-7408**
**1360 Harbor Drive
   (at Ash St.)**
Embarcadero, San Diego
See "Top Ten Restaurants of California," Pages 14-15.

LA CHAUMINE   **(714) 272-8540**
1466 Garnet Ave.
Pacific Beach, San Diego
   "The Cottage," very French and charming. Entrees prepared with expertise — delectable sauces, duck a l'orange, veal, langoustines, fish, lamb, beef and nightly specials include soup, salad and fresh vegetables. Good value.

Dinner: Every Night	Reservations Vital
Price: Moderate	Cards: AE, MC, V (BA)
Full Bar Service	Street Parking

CHRISTIAN'S DANISH INN   **(714) 462-4800**
8235 University Ave.
La Mesa
   A true dining experience, unhurried and delightful. Mr. Hansen is chef. Mrs. Hansen welcomes you with a glass of sherry. Daily changing Continental menu consists of *one* entree and includes appetizer, soup, vegetables, salad and homemade dessert. All lovingly prepared. "No Smoking Please."

Dinner: Tues.-Sat.	Reservations Essential
Prix Fixe: Expensive	Cards: MC, V (BA)
Wine and Beer	Parking Lot

FONTAINEBLEAU ROOM   **(714) 238-1818**
Little America Westgate Hotel
1055 Second Ave.
San Diego
   Authentic, beautiful French furnishings and decor. Attentive white-gloved waiters. Elegant dining. French menu. Our

recommendation, rack of lamb or chateaubriand (for two).
Three table d'hote selections, others a la carte.

Dinner: Every Night   Reservations Advised
Lunch: Mon.-Fri.   Major Cards
Brunch: Sun., 10-2   Garage Parking
 (Children's prices at Dress: Jackets
 Brunch)
Price: Expensive
Full Bar

MISTER A'S   (714) 239-1377
2550 Fifth Ave.
(at Laurel atop Financial Centre)
San Diego
Spectacular view of the city, harbor and Balboa Park — you can see forever! Lively, plush, Italiante. Extensive a la carte Continental menu. Favorites are Oysters Rockefeller, veal with gnocchi, and steaks. Generous portions. Excellent wine list. Pleasant for cocktails with view.

Dinner: Every Night   Reservations Advised
Lunch: Mon.-Fri.   Major Cards
Price: Expensive to Very Garage Parking
Full Bar   Dress: Jackets required

OLD TRIESTE   (714) 276-1841
2335 Morena Blvd.
San Diego
For fifteen years, owner/host Tommy has zealously served the finest Northern Italian cuisine. Ambrosial cannelloni and veal specialties. Excellent beef, seafood and squid. Complimentary fried zucchini. Soup or salad and pasta served with entree.

Dinner: Tues.-Sat.   Reservations Essential
Lunch: Tues.-Fri.   Major Cards
Price: Moderate to Expensive Parking Lot
Full Bar   Jacket at Dinner

PISCES   (714) 436-9362
7640 El Camino Real
La Costa Plaza
(entrance to Rancho La Costa)
Carlsbad
The most elegant restaurant in North San Diego County. Dramatic, glossy decor. Mirrors, crystal and candle-light. All seafood menu. Entrees like Lobster Thermidor in Cognac

sauce, served with vegetable and crunchy potato basket. Favorite dessert is fresh strawberries Grand Marnier. Impeccable service.

Dinner: Thurs.-Tues.	Reservations Definitely
(Closed Wednesday)	Cards: AE, MC, V(BA)
Price: Expensive to Very	Parking Lot
Full Bar	Dress: Jackets

PRINCE OF WALES GRILL   (714) 435-6611
Hotel del Coronado
1500 Orange Ave.
Coronado

English elegance steeped in the history of its namesake. A la carte Continental menu. Cart service. We recommend the Veal Oscar and chef's suggestions. Nicely presented drinks. Memorable.

Dinner: Every Night	Reservations Advised
Price: Expensive to Very	Cards: CB, MC, V(BA)
Full Bar	Validated Parking Lot

THEE BUNGALOW   (714) 224-2884
4966 West Point Loma Blvd.
Ocean Beach, San Diego

Cozy, country inn atmosphere. Chef-owner does marvelous things with duckling, veal and chicken. Soup, salad, fresh vegetables accompany entrees. Tempting desserts. Patio dining, weather permitting.

Dinner: Tues.-Sun.	Reservations Essential
Price: Moderate to Expensive	Cards: AE, MC, V(BA)
Wine and Beer	Small Parking Lot

TOP O' THE COVE   (714) 454-7779
1216 Prospect St.
La Jolla

Lovely 19th century La Jolla cottage above the cove. Continental favorites are beef tournedos and French onion soup. Entrees include fresh fruit compote, salad or soup, and vegetables. Ask for the day's specials. Excellent service.

Dinner: Tues.-Sun.	Reservations Recommended
Lunch: Tues.-Sat.	Cards: AE, MC, V(BA)
Brunch: Sun., 11-2	Street Parking
(Summer Only)	
Price: Expensive	
Full Bar	

TOP TEN SPECIALTY RESTAURANTS OF
GREATER SAN DIEGO

ALFONSO'S   **(714) 454-2232**
1251 Prospect St.
La Jolla
    A big, happy Mexican restaurant. Patio or inside dining by the fireplace. Traditional combinations served with rice and refried beans. Delicious sopes (little Mexican pizzas). Specialty is Carne Asada with salad. Luncheon daily specials are called "Alfonso's Secret."

Dinner and Lunch: Daily   Reservations: 6 or more
Lower Priced   Cards: AE, MC, V(BA)
Full Bar   Street Parking

Other Location:
Alfonso's East   **(714) 560-5388**
5252 Balboa Ave.
Clairemont

BULLY'S NORTH   **(714) 755-1660**
1404 Camino Del Mar
Del Mar
    Convivial and active. Best prime rib buy in town. Complete American menu includes salad, potatoes or rice. The Bully-burger and beef sandwiches are an entire meal. Good value.

Dinner: Every Night   No Reservations
Lunch: Mon.-Fri.   Cards: AE, MC, V(BA)
Price: Moderate   Street Parking
Full Bar

Other Locations:
Bully's   **(714) 459-2768**
5755 La Jolla Blvd.   Street Parking
La Jolla

Bully's East   **(714) 291-2665**
2401 Camino Del Rio South   Parking Lot
Mission Valley, San Diego

EL CHALAN   (714) 459-7707
5621 La Jolla Blvd.
Bird Rock Dist., La Jolla
    A cheerful, well-run Peruvian dining spot that features exotic Incan cookery. Ceviche, Pappas Rellenas (savory meat-stuffed potatoes), spicy marinated beef or duck, shredded chicken in cashew sauce and fish with rice.

Dinner: Wed.-Mon.	Reservations Accepted
(closed Tuesday)	Cards: AE, MC, V(BA)
Price: Moderate	Street Parking
Wine and Aperitifs	

THE CHART HOUSE   (714) 436-4044
2588 South Highway 101
Cardiff-by-the-Sea
    Impressive, multi-level structure on the beach...with a smashing ocean view. Good steaks, seafood and prime rib. Fine salad bar included. Friendly Bar/Lounge for cocktails.

Dinner: Every Night	Limited Reservations
Price: Moderate	Major Cards
Full Bar	Parking Lot

Other water-oriented locations:

2760 Shelter Island Dr.	**(714) 222-2216**
Shelter Island	
1270 Prospect St.	**(714) 459-8201**
La Jolla	
1701 Strand Way	**(714) 435-0155**
Coronado	

CHU DYNASTY   (714) 435-5300
1033 "B" Avenue
Coronado
    Mandarin food served with care by Chester Chu and family. Specialties such as whole Peking duck with pancakes make the trip across the bridge worth the toll. Order Chow San Shein, a delightful mix of beef, chicken, shrimp and vegetables.

Dinner: Tues.-Sun.	Reservations Suggested
Lunch: Tues.-Sat.	Cards: AE, MC, V(BA)
Lower Priced to Moderate	Parking Lot
Full Bar	

LA COSTA   (903) 385-8494
7th St. between Revolucion &
  Constitucion Aves.
Tijuana, B.C., Mexico

Just a block from the Jai Alai Palace, you'll find the best seafood restaurant in downtown Tijuana. Eighteen shrimp and nine lobster dishes. Good stuffed trout, Combinacion de Mariscos and tasty Costa Azul Shrimp. Dinners include appetizer, soup and rice. Menu in Spanish/English...prices, American dollars.

Dinner and Lunch Daily	No Reservations
Lower Priced to Moderate	Cards: MC, V(BA)
Full Bar	Street Parking

Other Location:
San Antonio Del Mar (ocean view)
14 miles south of the border on the
  Tijuana-Ensenada Toll Road

LA ESCONDIDA   (903) 386-2285
Ave. Santa Monica No. 1, Fracc. Las Palmas,
(Off Blvd. Agua Caliente, beyond Caliente Racetrack)
Tijuana, B.C., Mexico

Translated as "The Hideaway," this converted villa has a charming garden-view dining room and terrace for a Mexican-style change of pace. Menu, in English, offers peppered filet, fish and seasonal wild game.

Dinner and Lunch Daily	Reservations Accepted
Price: Moderate	Cards: DC, MC, V(BA)
Full Bar/Music Wed.-Sat.	Valet Parking or Parking Lot

HAMBURGUESA   (714) 295-0584
4016 Wallace St.
In Old Town State Historic Park
San Diego

This combination hamburger extravaganza and historical site is in San Diego's colorful "Old Town." Choose from 18 plump hamburgers, sip a frothy Margarita and turn time back to 1854 when the site was occupied by the notorious Jolly Boy Saloon. Interesting shops in adjacent Bazaar del Mundo.

Dinner and Lunch Daily	Limited Reservation Policy
Lower Priced	Cards: MC, V(BA)
Full Bar	Parking Lot

HOULIHAN'S OLD PLACE   (714) 297-6370
5223 Mission Center Rd.
Mission Valley, San Diego

Fun atmosphere. Jammed with interesting antiques, pictures and people. Favorite dishes are onion soup, stuffed shrimp, omelets, quiches. Daily specials. Hot dogs and burgers for kids. Cocktails in beer mugs (for big kids).

Dinner and Lunch Daily	Limited Reservation Policy
(continuous service)	Cards: AE, MC, V(BA)
Brunch: Sun., 10:30-2:30	Parking Lot
Lower Priced to Moderate	
Full Bar	

Other Locations: Encino, Long Beach, Newport Beach

LA MAISON DES PESCADOUX
2265 Bacon St.   **(714) 225-9579**
Ocean Beach, San Diego

Seafood prepared in the French manner by Chef Marcel Perrin...who headed the kitchen at San Francisco's La Bourgogne for 14 years. Personal selections: baked clams, quenelles with baby shrimp, Oysters Rockefeller. Also beef dishes and coq au vin.

Dinner: Mon.-Sat.	Reservations Recommended
Price: Moderate to Expensive	Cards: AE, MC, V(BA)
Full Bar Service	Parking Lot

CHEZ FELIX   (408) 373-0556
585 Cannery Row
Monterey

Tiny Chez Felix has a bay view from its upstairs perch. Start dinner with crab bisque or salad a l'ail. Seafood and meat are prepared with Provencal flair by the chef-owner. Superior dishes are salmon baked in parchment, sweetbreads and chicken Cynthia. Irresistible desserts.

Dinner: Tues.-Sun.	Reservations Essential
Price: Moderate to Expensive	Cards: MC, V (BA)
Wine	Street Parking

THE CLOCK GARDEN RESTAURANT
565 Abrego   **(408) 376-6100**
Monterey

The flower-filled brick patio here is a classy place for lunch or brunch. Be prepared for dinner items such as "topless tempters en casserole" (breasts of chicken), "little cuts all in a row — BBQ them and broil-ee-o" (pork tenderloin en brochette). All fun; popular.

Dinner: Every Night	Reservations Dinner Only
Lunch: Mon.-Fri.	Major Cards
Brunch: Sun., 10:30-2	Street Parking
Price: Moderate	
Full Bar	

LE COQ D'OR   (408) 624-4613
Mission and Fifth
Carmel

Carmel residents favor this charming little dinner house. Chicken in wine sauce, pork chops in sherry, salmon (in season) come with hearty soup and salad mimosa. A genuine "good deal" restaurant.

Dinner: Wed.-Mon.	Reservations Essential
(closed Tuesday)	No Credit Cards
Price: Moderate	Self Parking
Wine	

DEL MONTE LODGE   (408) 624-3811
Main Dining Room
3 mile N. of Carmel on "17 Mile Drive"
Pebble Beach

The view from this room, across a narrow Pebble Beach fairway to the Del Monte Peninsula-Carmel coastline, is among the most beautiful anywhere! Enormous full-course dinners are at fixed prices. Choice of several entrees. The most magnificent Easter Brunch we know is served in this lovely setting.

Dinner, Lunch, Breakfast:	Reservations Recommended
Daily	Cards: AE, MC, V(BA)
Price: Expensive	Valet Parking
Full Bar	

Other restaurant on premises:
Club XIX   (408) 625-1880

Same dramatic view. Best for lunch or brunch. Posh . . . expensive . . . formal for dinner.

Price: Expensive to Very	Reservations Recommended
Full Bar	Jacket and Tie at Dinner

L'ESCARGOT   (408) 624-4914
Mission & 4th Avenue
Carmel

L'Escargot is very French and very chic — with pewter, porcelain and copperware. The menu is short, but superb — chicken with cream and truffles, veal, steak poivre, a fresh fish daily. Escargot, but of course.

Dinner: Mon.-Sat.	Dinner by Reservation Only
Price: Expensive	No Credit Cards
Wine and Beer	Street Parking

NEPENTHE   (408) 667-2345
30 miles South of Carmel (on Cal. 1)
Big Sur

Dine on the terrace and revel in unsurpassed vistas of the Big Sur coastline. Marvelous spot for lunch, cocktails or dinner. Ambrosiaburgers, vegetarian salad, steak and baked chicken are specialties. Stop in the Phoenix Shop for local and imported handcrafts.

Dinner and Lunch Daily	Reservations Advised
Price: Moderate	Cards: AE, MC, V(BA)
Full Bar	Parking Area

PATISSERIE BOISSIERE   (408) 624-5008
Mission (between Ocean and 7th)
Carmel Plaza, Carmel

A perfect stop after a walk on the beach or tour of Carmel's shops and galleries. Indulge in French pastry or Quiche Lorraine accompanied by tea, coffee or wine. Good for light dinners. A stunning array of pastries, plus pate, to take out.

Dinner and Lunch:	No Reservations
Thurs.-Tues.	No Credit Cards
(closed Wed. and the	Street Parking
month of November)	
Lower Priced to Moderate	
Wine and Beer	

RAFFAELLO   (408) 624-1541
Mission (between Ocean and 7th)
Carmel

Raffaello's magnificent Northern Italian food is prepared by Amelia d'Agliano. Son Remo is host. The menu lists four pastas, six ways with veal, five with chicken. Or try the Dover sole stuffed with prawns. A memorable dining experience.

Dinner: Wed.-Mon.	Reservations Essential
(closed Tuesday)	Cards: MC
Price: Moderate to Expensive	Parking Lot
Wine and Beer	

THE SARDINE FACTORY   (408) 373-3775
701 Wave St.
Cannery Row, Monterey
See "Top Ten Restaurants of California," Pages 22-23.

WHALING STATION INN   (408) 373-3778
763 Wave St.
Cannery Row, Monterey

An old Chinese grocery was renovated and filled with antiques and nostalgia. Owner John Pistos serves the freshest available fish and has fine California wines. Several good meat dishes, but we like the seafood Italian-style.

Dinner: Every Night	Reservations Recommended
Lunch: Mon.-Fri.	Major Cards
Price: Moderate	Parking Lot
Full Bar	

CHINA CAMP   (916) 441-7966
1015 The Embarcadero
Old Sacramento

   Operated by the sons of the venerable Frank Fat, China Camp is built on four dining levels in a renovated river front building. The menu is a combination of Chinese and American dishes. "Chinese Oven Discoveries" include oven fried ribs and wok pepper steak. We like Drunk Steak and Spirited Chicken.

Dinner: Every Night	No Reservations
Lunch: Mon.-Fri.	Cards: AE, MC, V(BA)
Price: Moderate	Parking Lot
Full Bar	

D. O. MILLS   (916) 442-1866
111 "K" Street
Old Sacramento

   Housed in a historic three-story building, it is the ultimate "theme" restaurant. Furnished with authentic artifacts of an 1800's banking house. Victorian bar, banking memorabilia, period furniture. A short blackboard menu features excellent steaks sold by the ounce. Interesting place for children.

Dinner: Every Night	No Reservations
Lunch: Mon.-Sat.	Cards: AE, MC, V(BA)
Price: Moderate	Parking Lot
Full Bar	

FIREHOUSE   (916) 442-4772
1112 Second
   (between K and L Sts.)
Old Sacramento

   Restored from a real firehouse originally built in 1853. Decor is "Late 19th Century Elegant." Continental-American dinner menu. Specialties: spinach salad, chateaubriand, roasted wild boar (24-hour notice), buffalo steak when available.

Dinner: Mon.-Sat.	Reservations Advised
Lunch: Mon.-Fri.	Cards: MC, V(BA)
Price: Expensive	Parking Lot
Full Bar	

FRANK FAT'S   (916) 442-7092
806 "L" Street
Sacramento

Frank Fat's is unique and a Capitol favorite featuring authentic Cantonese food and American steaks. Delicious Chinese hors d'oeuvres are the Yuk Kwok, paper wrapped chicken and barbecue pork slices. We like asparagus steak, N.Y. steak with oyster sauce and The Clams. For dessert have Frank's great banana cream pie.

Dinner: Mon.-Sat.	Reservations Advised
Lunch: Mon.-Fri.	Cards: AE, MC, V(BA)
Price: Moderate to Expensive	Self Parking
Full Bar	

GOLDEN ACORN   (209) 745-2363
805 Crystal Way
(off Hwy. 99 — take Fairway Drive turnoff)
Galt

The Golden Acorn is quiet, softly-lit and comfortable. The fare is Italian. The complete dinner (21 to choose from) begins with minestrone, then salad and hors d'oeuvres. Generous servings of Veal Parmigiana, Scalloppini Genovese and Saltimbocca.

Dinner: Tues.-Sat.	Reservations Accepted
Price: Moderate	No Credit Cards
Full Bar	Parking Lot

JIM AND DENNY'S   (916) 443-9655
12th and Terminal Way
Sacramento

Jim and Denny's may manufacture California's best hamburger. This tiny diner is always packed at lunchtime. Fun to take out your burger and munch it under a tree in Capitol Park. Your kids will like it, too.

Hours: 5AM-4PM	No Reservations
Lower Priced	No Credit Cards
No Liquor	

ROSEMOUNT GRILL   (916) 455-5387
3145 Folsom Blvd. and Fwy. 80
Sacramento

Businessmen, senior citizens, teenagers and politicians all pour into this restaurant. Good food in a folksy atmosphere at a modest price. Counter and booth service. Clam chowder, steaks and chops are recommended. Large martinis.

Dinner and Lunch Daily   No Reservations
Price: Moderate   No Credit Cards
Full Bar   Parking Lot

RESTAURANT LA SALLE   (916) 927-1161
943 Howe Avenue
Sacramento

Richard Vickers is chef-owner and he changes much of the menu from day to day. Soup may be hot or icy cold, salads are determined by the same "whatever-I-feel-like-making" approach. Recommended entrees are sea bass Florentine, sauteed frogs legs, Beef Wellington (for two) and sweetbreads in a marvelous sauce. Fine wine list.

Dinner & Lunch: Tues.-Sat.   Reservations Recommended
Price: Moderate   Cards: MC, V(BA)
Full Bar   Self Parking

THE JACK'S DEER CREEK PLAZA
101 Broad St.   (916) 265-5808
Nevada City

An interesting turn-of-the-century building overlooking Deer Creek. "The Jacks" is Victorian . . . a quality country restaurant. An outdoor deck for dining in spring and summer. Dinner includes hors d'oeuvre tray, soup, salad (sprouts, almonds, lettuce), and dessert parfait. Varied entrees.

Dinner: Mon.-Sat.   Reservations Advised
Lunch: Mon.-Fri.   Cards: AE, MC, V(BA)
Price: Moderate   Parking Lot
Full Bar

WULFF'S   (916) 922-8575
2333 Fair Oaks Blvd.
Sacramento

A French restaurant that shines above the others. Main dishes prove the creativity in the kitchen . . . curried lamb in crepes, rabbit cooked in white wine, duck in cream sauce. Daily specials. A superb value, too!

Dinner: Tues.-Sat.   Reservations Recommended
Lunch: Tues.-Fri.   Cards: AE, MC, V(BA)
   (closed last 2 weeks July) Parking Lot
Price: Moderate
Full Bar

LAS CASUELAS NUEVAS   **(714) 328-8844**
70050 Highway 111
Restaurant Row, Rancho Mirage
    A Mexican hacienda in the desert. The menu folder looks like it contains a land grant . . . it offers 14 complete dinners, numerous a la carte, Especialidades de Casa *and* children's plates. Grande Margaritas.

Dinner and Lunch Daily	No Reservations
Brunch: Sun., 10-3	Major Cards
Price: Moderate	Valet Parking
Full Bar	

Original Location:
368 N. Palm Canyon Drive   **(714) 325-3213**
Palm Springs

CHEZ FRANCOISE   **(714) 325-7355**
267 N. Palm Canyon Drive
Palm Springs
    A very good French restaurant. Francoise runs it with friendly efficiency. She offers daily specials, plus 10 a la carte entrees. Splurge on a luscious dessert souffle. Early Bird Dinners (4:30-6:30) and an outdoor terrace.

Dinner and Lunch Daily	Reservations Accepted
Price: Moderate to Expensive	Major Cards
Full Bar	Valet Parking

MARIO'S   **(714) 325-9172**
217 N. Palm Canyon Drive
Palm Springs
    A happy, music-filled place serving large Italian dinners. Children and grownups alike enjoy the lively atmosphere. Hard to beat value for informal fun and food.

Dinner: Tues.-Sun.	Reservations Recommended
Lower Priced to Moderate	Major Cards
Wine and Beer	Self Parking

NATE'S DELI   (714) 325-3506
283 N. Palm Canyon Drive
Palm Springs

Nate's menu lists 100 different sandwiches...including super-sized corned beef or pastrami with sauerkraut, pickles and relishes. Good deal is the Early Diner's Special, daily from 4-6 PM. There's something here for everyone, from Grandpa to the kids.

Dinner, Lunch, Breakfast:	Reservations Accepted
Daily	Cards: MC, V(BA)
Lower Priced to Moderate	Easy Self Parking
Wine and Beer	

THE NEST   (714) 346-2314
75-188 Highway 111
Indian Wells

The Nest is one of the best values in this area. Mostly Italian and French...dishes range from ravioli to sweetbreads. One entree is listed, "Ask What The Help Ate." A favorite with local folk, tourists (and the help).

Dinner: Tues.-Sun.	Reservations Advised
Price: Moderate	Cards: MC, V(BA)
Wine and Beer	Self Parking

THE OLD WORLD   (714) 325-5502
262 S. Palm Canyon Drive
Palm Springs

Intimate inside, out front the patio is a Palm Springs' sidewalk cafe. Omelettes, waffles, salads, sandwiches and homemade soup. Big eaters favor the Belgian Brunch. A second floor restaurant serves fine prime rib.

Dinner and Lunch Daily	Reservations Suggested
Price: Moderate	Cards: AE, MC, V(BA)
Wine and Beer	Parking in Rear

THE RUBAIYAT   (714) 325-1301
Sheraton-Oasis Hotel
155 S. Belardo Road
Palm Springs

We like the Rubaiyat room for a complete evening — cocktails, dinner, dancing. Continental menu and a good salad bar. Excellent prime rib roasted in rock salt, shish kebab, seafood and roast specialties. Outdoor terrace dining.

Dinner, Lunch, Breakfast: Reservations Recommended
    Daily   Major Cards
Price: Moderate   Valet Parking
Full Bar

THE SUNSHINE MEAT, FISH   (714) 346-5641
AND LIQUOR CO.
Highway 111 at Portola
Palm Desert

The answer for fans of steak and seafood combinations. Also a la carte prime rib, lots of fish, broiled steaks, stuffed potatoes, artichokes. Salads, sandwiches and hot dishes for lunch. Young, mellow mood. Usually packed between 7 and 9 PM.

Dinner: Every Night   No Reservations
Lunch: Mon.-Fri.   Cards: MC, V(BA)
Price: Moderate   Self Parking
Full Bar

Another Location:
440 S. Palm Canyon Drive   (714) 325-2388
Palm Springs

TRANSYLVANIA   (714) 346-3266
Palms to Pines Plaza
72-820 El Paseo
Palm Desert

Don't let the name frighten you away...nor the Dracula cocktail. An interesting spot serving Romanian food. Tempting specials are Shish Kebab, Golden Hen Breast Pilaf and Mititei (Romanian beef sausage). Early Dinner deal, 4-6 PM. American dishes for non-Transylvanians.

Dinner: Tues.-Sun.	Reservations Accepted
Price: Moderate	Cards: MC, V(BA)
Full Bar	Parking Lot

LE VALLAURIS   (714) 325-5059
385 W. Tahquitz-McCullum Wy.
  (West of Palm Canyon Drive)
Palm Springs

Le Vallauris, the desert son of a chic L.A. restaurant, serves premium French food. We're told that due to zoning laws they operate as a private club. The public is admitted for a $5.00 one-visit charge. If you can dig this and you hunger for classic cuisine, it's a fine choice. Pleasant for luncheon. Patio dining.

Dinner & Lunch: Tues.-Sun.	Reservations Essential
Price: Expensive to Very	Cards: MC, V(BA)
Full Bar	Valet Parking

INDEX

121

123

Mexican
Barragan's, 56
Cano's, 49
El Chavo, 49
El Gato, 59

Russian
Kavkaz, 50

Seafood
Amelia's, 34
Bernard's, 24-25, 28, 31
Calabasas Inn, 43
Cano's, 49
Crab Cooker, 43
Delaney's Kettle of Fish, 52
Delaney's Sea Shanty, 43
Galley Steak House, 41
Millie Rierra's Seafood Grotto, 44
Nantucket Light, 44
Noel's, 44
The Pelican, 45
Pelican's Catch, 44
The Pelican's Roost, 45
Le Quai, 45
The Saloon, 42
Sand Castle, 45
Scandia, 10-11, 30, 39
The Seashell, 30, 45
Walt's Wharf, 58

Spanish
La Masia, 50

Swiss
Le Petite Swiss, 57
St. Moritz, 39

Thai
Bangkok 1 Restaurant, 46

Yugoslavian
The Paragon, 51

**TYPES OF FOOD
SAN FRANCISCO BAY AREA**

American
The Beginning, 78
Bill's Place, 92
The Broken Egg Omelet House, 92
Brennan's, 92
The Buena Vista, 98
Canlis', 78
Le Creole, 78
The Elegant Farmer, 79
The Garret, 93
The Golden Eagle, 96
Grison's, 79
Gulliver's, 79
The Iron Works, 79
The Leopard, 80
MacArthur Park, 80
Mama's, 26-27, 65, 80
Marie Callender's, 53
Norman's, 76
The Nut Tree, 100

Pam Pam East, 94
Sam's Grill, 94
Sear's Fine Food, 94
Tadich Grill, 20-21, 67, 84
Upstart Crow & Co., 97
What This Country Needs, 94

Chinese
Asia Garden, 88
China Station, 85
Kee Joon's, 85
The Mandarin, 86
Nam Yuen, 86
North China Restaurant, 87
Tao Tao Cafe, 87
Trader Vic's, 67, 77
Yank Sing, 88
Yet Wah, 68, 88

Continental
Cafe Biarritz, 95
Blue Fox, 75
Carnelian Room, 98
Le Club, 75
Doro's, 65, 72
Fournou's Ovens, 65, 75
La Hacienda, 75
Narsai's, 66, 76
Norman's, 76
Rolf's, 76
Soupcon, 77
Trader Vic's, 67, 77

Czechoslovakian
Vlasta's European Inn, 91

English
The Coachman, 95
Monroe's, 90

French
Chez Jon, 70
Chez Joseph, 70
Chez Leon, 95
Le Club, 75
Cow Hollow Inn, 69
La Croisette, 69
Le Cyrano, 69
Domain Chandon, 99
La Mirabelle, 66, 71
L'Orangerie, 8-9, 66, 71
La Potiniere, 71
La Quiche, 94
La Terrasse, 71

German
Schroeder's, 96

Hungarian
Paprika's Fono, 90
Vlasta's European Inn, 91

Indian
Gaylord, 89